# SCRIPTWRITING

## MA Creative Writing Anthologies 2014

UEA SCRIPTWRITING ANTHOLOGY 2014

First published by Egg Box Publishing 2014



A CIP record for this book is available from the British Library.

UEA Scriptwriting Anthology 2014 is typeset in Caslon. Titles are set in Din condensed, with subtitles in Gotham.

Printed and bound in the UK by Imprint Digital.

Designed and typeset by Sean Purdy.

Proofread by Sarah Gooderson.

Distributed by Central Books.

ISBN: 9780957661172

# ACKNOWLEDGEMENTS

Thanks are due to the School of Literature, Drama and Creative Writing at UEA in partnership with Egg Box Publishing for making this anthology possible.

We'd also like to thank the following people:

Trezza Azzopardi, Amit Chaudhuri, Andrew Cowan, Giles Foden, Sarah Gooderson, Lavinia Greenlaw, Rachel Hore, Kathryn Hughes, James Lasdun, Daniel Leeson, Michael Lengsfield, Frances Leviston, Jean McNeil, Natalie Mitchell, Beatrice Poubeau, Sophie Robinson, Helen Smith, Henry Sutton, Val Taylor, Steve Waters, Peter Womack and Toby Young.

Nathan Hamilton at Egg Box Publishing and Sean Purdy.

Editorial team:

Michelle Brown<br>
Susan K Burton<br>
Niall Cunniffe<br>
John Dennehy<br>
Hannah Coneys<br>
Affly Johnson<br>
Ella Micheler<br>
Lauren Razavi<br>
Anealla Safdar<br>
Rebecca White

# CONTENTS

## Introduction



## Contributors

# VAL TAYLOR

## Introduction

'Nothing, like something, happens anywhere.' In *I Remember, I Remember*, Philip Larkin reminds us of the intimate connection between action, place and memory; between what happens, where it happens, and how it is remembered. Or, in his elegant paradox, nothing happens. (Samuel Beckett's *Waiting for Godot* was famously reviewed in similarly paradoxical terms following its British première, as a play in which 'nothing happens, twice.')

Larkin's paradox is an essentially dramatic premise, and it's one with which we engage from the outset of the MA in Creative Writing: Scriptwriting. In our reading, we begin with a story's 'world' (or worlds): with place and time; inhabitants, visitors and interlopers; with habitual occurrences and extraordinary irruptions. In our writing, we ask our characters to make, unmake and remake their world/s through deeds and words, to be made or remade by them, and to share their responses with us. But as Larkin shows, while we look for actions and events, we should recognise what doesn't happen, what our characters don't do; for they happen at the same time, in the same place. The boundary between the two – between something and nothing – is where drama resides.

The scriptwriters in this collection locate their stories in very different places: in Paris, Liverpool, or an Essex car park. In a shopping mall decked out for Christmas, or a boarding school in a futuristic 'Yorkshire Dales Botanical Park'. A fast-food takeaway on a busy urban street, a seaside joke shop, or a haunted house. On a countryside railway bridge, or a Greek island.

What happens there? (Or not.) I'll let Michelle and Harry, Stephan and Monte, Phil and Eliot, Olivia and Ruth, and our two Nicks, show you that. These stories are their responses to Larkin's paradox.

**Val Taylor**
**Director of the MA in Scriptwriting**

# MICHELLE BROWN

## Maya's Order

EXT. STREET – NIGHT

A grimy-looking street. Lined with various shops: Afro-Caribbean takeouts, betting venues, derelict social clubs. A CLUB PROMOTER stands in the middle of the street handing out leaflets to PASSERS-BY.

CLUB PROMOTER

Traffic light party at the Honey Club tonight! Wear red if you're taken, yellow if you're undecided and green if you're single! I guarantee you will find true love tonight!

INT. CHICKEN AND CHIPS SHOP – NIGHT

The shop buzzes with CUSTOMERS, both young and old.

The EMPLOYEES, dressed in a hideous mustard-coloured uniform, work tirelessly to serve the hungry customers who bombard the counter. A LARGE WOMAN with a strong Latino accent does her best to explain exactly what she wants over the noise.

AARON, 17, hands an ELDERLY WOMAN her tray of food. He's cute, in a geeky sort of way.

The Elderly Woman moves away from the till making way for the next customer: AMELIA, 16. Plain and simple. She grins at Aaron, revealing her train-track braces. Amelia slides her braids over her shoulder in a poor attempt to look attractive.

AMELIA
Hi, Aaron! I didn't know you were working tonight! Sucks on a Friday night, what with school and that.

Aaron forces a smile. He looks up at the clock anxiously.

AARON
Uh, what can I—

AMELIA
All that homework too. How'd you manage? What Ms Heath gave us for English today seems like it'll be tough—

AARON
Amelia. Eating in or taking out?

AMELIA
Eating in. Definitely.

AARON
What can I get you?

Amelia squints at the colourful menu of burgers, chips and kebabs. Standing behind her is a BURLY MAN with a retreating hairline. He folds his arms. Huffs impatiently.

AMELIA
I dunno. They all look the same without my glasses. Amelia points to her face.

AMELIA (CONT'D)
Did you notice?

Aaron glances up at the clock. He's becoming more irritated by the second.

AARON
Sorry, Amelia, but I really need you to order.

AMELIA
You suggest something.

AARON
The beefburger meal with small chips and a drink of your choice is the cheapest. If that helps.

Amelia smiles.

AMELIA
I'll go for that then. You're so sma—

AARON
That's £2.50, Amelia.

Amelia looks hurt. She delves into her purse and brings out a handful of coins. Aaron looks miserably at her as she takes out one coin at a time, counting as she goes.

Aaron stares up at the slowly ticking clock.

Amelia holds out the coins to Aaron, who wastes no time in collecting it. Their hands touch and Amelia holds on longer than normal.

Aaron pulls away.

AMELIA

Hope that's the right amount—

AARON

It's fine.

Aaron slides open the till. Dumps the coins in. Slams it shut and disappears into the kitchen.

Amelia sighs after him. Gooey-eyed. She reaches into her bag and pulls out a light pink card which reads: 'AARON'.

Aaron returns to the counter with Amelia's order in hand. Amelia makes a move to give him the card.

AMELIA

Aaron, I didn't get a chance to—

Aaron holds her tray out to her.

AARON

Enjoy. Next!

Amelia drops the card into her bag sadly. Reluctant to take her tray. She looks back at Aaron, who is now attending to the Burly Man.

Amelia sits at a table, closest to Aaron's till. She watches him as he mechanically carries out his order.

The shop doors open wide. In walks MAYA, 17, attractive, looks more like 21, with her friends, OLIVIA, 16, and SIENNA, 17. Heads turn their way as they glide past. Amelia throws them a dirty look.

Aaron's face immediately lights up as he spots Maya.

EMPLOYEE #1

Next please!

Maya is about to go over to the employee, when Aaron puts his hand up.

AARON

I've got this one!

He smiles proudly at Maya.

AARON (CONT'D)

Evening.

MAYA

Hey. You all right?

AARON

As all right as I can be on a Friday night in this place.

MAYA

True. God knows I'd hate myself if I had to work here. No offence to you or anything. Just me.

She grins at him.

MAYA (CONT'D)

I'll have a—

AARON

Double cheeseburger, medium fries, Fanta, no ice.

Olivia and Sienna exchange looks.

MAYA

Right.

Maya is baffled.

AARON

What? You're here every Friday night, usual time, usual order. You keep us in business with your weekly visits.

Olivia coughs, interrupting the pair.

AARON (CONT'D)

Sorry, what will you be having?

Aaron takes Olivia's and Sienna's orders and their payment.

AARON (CONT'D)

I'll be right with you.

Maya turns her attention to her friends as Aaron leaves.

OLIVIA

So this is why you're in here every Friday. Because of Greasy Fingers back there?

Amelia scowls. How dare they call him that?

OLIVIA (CONT'D)

The boy knows your damn order when Ricardo didn't even know your favourite colour.

Sienna laughs.

MAYA

Don't be mean, man. He's cool.

Amelia scowls the more.

MAYA (CONT'D)

And no, I don't come here for him. I come here

because it's a Friday. Ain't no one wanna be cooking on a Friday night.

Aaron places drinks onto a tray.

MAYA (CONT'D)

Thanks.

Aaron disappears into the kitchen once more.

OLIVIA

Friday night. Valentine's Day and we're up in here like a sad group of old women when Aisha and them lot are partying. If you wanted cheering up then this ain't the way to go about it. I don't do all that sitting-down-drowning-your-sorrows shit. You get out there and you get yourself a new man. Show that fool of a boy what he's missing.

Maya scoffs.

MAYA

I ain't missing him! He's been on my case ever since begging me to get back with him, like that's ever going to happen.

Aaron returns and puts two bags of chips on the tray.

MAYA (CONT'D)

Boys are idiots.

Maya looks up at Aaron.

AARON

Two small chips for you two—

MAYA
Not you, of course.

AARON
Sorry?

MAYA
You're not an idiot.

Sienna raises her eyebrows at Aaron as he beams at Maya.

AARON
Good to know.

Aaron goes back to complete the order.

SIENNA
Seriously, what's with you two? I'm starting to think there's more to your weekly visits here, May.

OLIVIA
Now I get why you dumped Ricardo. You were doing the dirty on him with Greasy Fingers.

MAYA
Oh shut up.

Aaron carries Maya's order proudly.

AARON
And one medium for you—

He places the box down in front of Maya. Flashes a smile. All teeth on show.

Maya picks at her chips.

AARON (CONT'D)
Hold on a sec. You'll be needing ketchup with that.

Aaron bends down under his till.

OLIVIA
So when are you two gonna admit that you've been seeing each other this whole time?

MAYA
Seriously. Shush. You're both tripping. He ain't even my type. He's far from it.

Amelia smiles to herself. Pops a chip into her mouth. Silently pleased.

Aaron's face pokes up from behind the till. His smile has disappeared. He dumps a handful of ketchup, salt and napkins onto the tray.

AARON (FLATLY)
Enjoy.

Maya leads the girls to an empty table next to Amelia.

Aaron turns his attention to his next customer. His face hard, his lips pressed together tightly. It is another OLD PERSON.

AARON (CONT'D)
Can I help?

INT. CHICKEN AND CHIPS SHOP – LATER

The shop is a little quieter now, with the odd customer ordering. Amelia sucks away on an empty drink carton, watching Aaron's every move. She pulls out the card and slips it onto her tray.

Aaron wipes down a few tables keeping a close eye on Maya who is still at the table with her friends. Maya slurps her drink, mocking being drunk.

She sighs.

MAYA
I am done with guys. Honestly.

SIENNA
Ricardo was fine, though. If it wasn't for the whole girl code thing, I'd have tapped that.

MAYA
Sienna!

OLIVIA
She does have a point. Ricardo is fine. Half god, half human.

MAYA
You're just concentrating on looks. He's a dick deep down. It was only ever about sex with him. Serious. I'll be like, let's watch a movie, he'll be like 'does it have sex in it?'

Amelia winces as the conversation goes on.

MAYA (CONT'D)
I'd want to walk in the park on a nice summer's day and he'd ask, 'why, do you want to do it in the park?' I swear there was never a conversation we had where sex wasn't involved somehow.

OLIVIA
Why are you so surprised? Do you think he wants to sit and talk about his future with you?

Boys are physical, Maya. It's all they know.

SIENNA

It's all they want to know.

MAYA

Exactly. One of these days, it'll be nice to have a guy who would love to just talk, rather than grind on me all night at some sleazy club and take me home afterwards. Is that too much to ask?

Olivia and Sienna look at each other. Then back at Maya.

OLIVIA

Course it is. Guys like that don't exist.

SIENNA

Not round here, anyway.

Olivia takes a sip from her drink.

OLIVIA

I still say, we go out tonight. The night is young, and, as much fun as it was talking about all this heartfelt stuff, I would much rather be in a club.

Olivia gets to her feet.

OLIVIA (CONT'D)

You coming or what?

Sienna shrugs her shoulders at Maya apologetically.

MAYA

Fine.

The girls pick up their belongings and head for the door.

Amelia gets up from her seat and goes towards Aaron. This is her moment.
Maya smiles at him as she walks past.

MAYA (CONT'D)
See you around.

Aaron drops the cleaning cloth on the table.

AARON
Wait a minute!

Aaron races to the till, ignoring any sort of health and safety measures. Ignoring Amelia. He reappears a few seconds later, straightening up a rumpled hot red envelope. He holds it out to Maya, who reaches out for it confused as to what it is.

Amelia's face crumples. She stands awkwardly in the background.

AARON (CONT'D)
Sorry about the...

Aaron gestures wildly to the wrinkled card.

Maya tears it open. Olivia and Sienna giggle behind her.

AARON (CONT'D)
I know I'm just 'Greasy Fingers'—

Olivia stops laughing. Looks away, embarrassed.

AARON (CONT'D)
—And not your type – I believe 'far from it' were your exact words...

Maya looks over the card.

AARON (CONT'D)
But for what it's worth, I think you are amazing. You're pretty, funny, kind and sweet...

Maya shuts the card slowly and looks up at Aaron. He shifts uncomfortably on the spot.

AARON (CONT'D)
Any guy would be lucky to have you. I hope you find one who will treat you right and give you the love and care you deserve.

He smiles at her.

AARON (CONT'D)
Happy Valentine's Day.

Maya tiptoes slightly and plants a soft kiss on Aaron's cheek.

MAYA
See you next Friday?

Aaron's mouth drops open. Shocked.

Maya and her friends leave giggling amongst themselves.

Amelia flings her card at a nearby bin. Unknown to her she misses completely.

Aaron stands rooted to the spot. Unable to process what has just happened. Amelia rushes past him.

AARON
Hey, Amelia, have a good night!

EXT. CHICKEN AND CHIPS SHOP – NIGHT

An upset Amelia pauses and stares into the window.

Aaron walks back to the till. He spots the scrunched up envelope on the floor and picks it up. Amelia is confused. Didn't she put it in the bin? She clutches onto her bag as she watches Aaron turn the card over. Hopeful.

Aaron opens the card. He scans through its contents at what seems to be lightning speed. He closes the card. Holds it for a few seconds. Then...

He slots it into the bin and walks off with a spring in his step.

AMELIA

Dick!

Amelia storms off down the road. She waves the annoying Club Promoter out of her face as he offers her a leaflet.

THE END.

**Michelle Brown** was born in London, England to Nigerian migrants. As a child she filled countless notebooks with stories and later decided to pursue a career in writing. Michelle is particularly interested in writing for young people and Nigerian audiences.

# NICHOLAS COHEN

## First Person

*An extract from a comedy feature film*

**<u>OPENING CREDITS SEQUENCE</u>**

INT. BROOKLYN CAFÉ. DAWN

Lean, intelligent, haggard DANIEL SHRIVER (32) sits at an empty table finishing his coffee. He stares at the empty seat opposite him where another cup of coffee and Danish sit completely untouched. DANIEL speaks quietly to the empty chair.

DANIEL

You know I could really do with one of your dumb jokes.

Burly, red-haired, pierced ROSIE (34) sweeps by and picks up DANIEL's empty cup. She stands by DANIEL and joins him in staring at the empty seat and untouched coffee.

ROSIE

He was always late. I remember that. Every time.

ROSIE claps DANIEL's shoulder forcefully in solidarity. DANIEL makes to pay.

ROSIE

What is that? Is that real money in your hand? I must be dreaming.

ROSIE bats DANIEL's hand away.

ROSIE

Pay me when you're rich and famous.

DANIEL

Don't hold your breath.

ROSIE

What am I – an idiot? Do I look like I'm holding my breath?

DANIEL stands. In a moment of private ritual he holds the table by the untouched coffee and shuts his eyes, remembering his dead brother. He opens his eyes and heads off.

ROSIE

Be good Daniel. And bring me back some native women. I'm sick of these New York bitches. (Spotting a skinny businesswoman) Why good morning, ma'am. (Smiling flirtatiously) How are you today?

INT. NEW YORK CAB. DAWN

DANIEL sits quietly in the cab. He opens his bag and examines his new DSLR CAMERA. The CAB DRIVER chats away. DANIEL is not listening.

EXT. NEW YORK STREETS. DAWN

DANIEL records an answerphone greeting staring out. Even at dawn every kind of person is moving. COPS, COMMUTERS, the HOMELESS, STREET VENDORS. DANIEL's voice is flat as though from a great distance.

DANIEL
Hey it's Daniel. I'm out of the city on a kinda... job... thing. You can email me I guess...

INT. CAB. DAWN

DANIEL shoots the SUNRISE waking the city. He shoots STREET DANCERS. A STREET PREACHER declaiming, HASSIDS jostling past DELIVERY MEN.

An ELVIS LOOKALIKE (56) leads an outdoor AEROBIC ELVIS BOOT CAMP and has a group of ELDERLY FITNESS FANATICS shakin' all over.

A YOUNG BOY (5) munching a huge hotdog has a face smeared with mustard and goo. He grins at DANIEL and opens his mouth displaying uneaten sausage.

END CREDITS

INT. AIRPLANE. DAY

DANIEL is still filming as he sits by RON (50), a fastidious businessman who carefully lays out travel pillow, eyeshades and hand cream then turns and covers the lens.

RON
Hey! It is completely illegal to film in here!

DANIEL
Sorry. I forget.

RON regards dishevelled DANIEL with alarm and disapproval.

DANIEL
It's not like I'm a terrorist. I may look like a terrorist but really I just need a shave.

RON is not so sure. He turns, hiding in a newspaper. DANIEL is embarrassed to spot a FAMILY in the aisle also watching him. He packs the camera and shuts his eyes.

INT. AIRPLANE. DAY

The plane hits tarmac. DANIEL jolts awake, dazzled by sharp Mediterranean sun. The journey has compounded his dishevellment – he looks really raggedy.

INT. ATHENS AIRPORT. DAY

DANIEL passes large totally clouded-up SMOKING ROOMS resembling steam baths. Amidst modern security and shops prowl ELDERLY LOTTERY TOUTS with TICKET BELTS slung over their shoulders like ammunition declaiming in musical voices.

INT. ATHENS AIRPORT LOBBY. DAY

DANIEL scans names on the WELCOME CARDS displayed in arrivals. None are him. He extracts his CELLPHONE.

As he dials he looks around. Fast asleep on a bench is a short and skinny pale man GEORGIOS (21) holding a card that reads 'DANIEL SHREYEVERE.' DANIEL approaches and gently nudges GEORGIOS.

GEORGIOS
Mm?

DANIEL
Me. I am Daniel.

GEORGIOS
Daniel Shreeveeree? You? Daniel Shreeveerreee?

DANIEL
Shriver. Daniel Shriver.

GEORGIOS
OK. Daniel Shreeveerree. Good news. Come please.

GEORGIOS leads DANIEL away.

EXT. AIRPORT CARPARK BACKLOT. DAY

Leaning on a filthy FORD FIESTA is LEFTERIS (56), a burly handsome-faced man whose belly is spilling out of his yellow T-shirt. LEFTERIS's salt-and-pepper hair is tied back in a ponytail.

LEFTERIS
Daniel Shriver! Welcome to the Hellenic Republic of Greece.

DANIEL
Thanks.

LEFTERIS
I am Lefteris. This is my Athenian assistant Georgios.

DANIEL shakes hands with both men.

LEFTERIS
I am the manager of Yannis's resort. You will have a wonderful time filming I am sure. Now you should turn the camera on and film me.

DANIEL
Uh... Yannis told me just to film the resort and the island. It's a promo.

LEFTERIS
Yannis does not know about films. Turn the camera on and film me.

DANIEL
Why?

LEFTERIS
You will see. Follow me please.

EXT. ATHENS AIRPORT TERMINAL ENTRANCE. DAY

SECURITY GUARDS suspiciously eye LEFTERIS and DANIEL, now filming him.

LEFTERIS
Better to be quick when you are shooting me here.

DANIEL
Why are we even doing this?

LEFTERIS
OK quick. (Grinning broadly at the camera) Welcome to Athens! Here we are at the international airport. Many people know about the troubles here in Greece. But also there are many myths. Look around – do you see gangs of young people throwing bombs? Do you see police shooting in the streets? Turn the camera around. Have a look!

DANIEL pans his camera. It settles on a CONFUSED GERMAN FAMILY. LEFTERIS barks at GEORGIOS, grins at the GERMAN FAMILY and gives them a double thumbs up. The GERMAN FAMILY hurry off, disturbed.

LEFTERIS

So peaceful.

An AIRPORT SECURITY GUARD lumbers over.

LEFTERIS

Camera off.

THE SECURITY GUARD fiercely questions LEFTERIS in Greek. LEFTERIS shrugs and pleads.

LEFTERIS, THE SECURITY GUARD and GEORGIOS all talk at once over each other.

A small crowd gathers – an ANCIENT LOTTERY TOUT approaches DANIEL and starts talking animatedly in Greek. DANIEL tries to ignore him.

THE GUARD demands to see the footage. He grabs the camera and reviews it. He smiles and shakes his head indicating that they are all crazy.

The crowd disperses. All except for the ANCIENT LOTTERY TOUT who continues talking to DANIEL in Greek. He shakes DANIEL's hand warmly.

INT. ATHENIAN CAR. DAY

DANIEL snoozes as LEFTERIS drives through the FREEWAY.

LEFTERIS

DANIEL! Daniel! Turn the camera on!

DANIEL

Why?

LEFTERIS

Filming.

DANIEL
Filming what? The freeway? We have those in the United States.

LEFTERIS
Greek infrastructure. Point the camera at me.

DANIEL
Lefteris. This is ludicrous.

LEFTERIS
If you are too tired for your job, give me the camera. We stop and I film myself.

DANIEL
Keep your eyes on the road.

Reluctantly DANIEL switches the CAMERA on.

LEFTERIS
Kaleemera. Here you see the Greek infrastructure functioning just like Manhattan and Washington DC. Despite economic troubles we won't let the show come off the road. People say Romans built the first straight roads. What madness? Everything Roman was stolen from Greece. Same as today. Just ask Silvio Berlusconi.

DANIEL
OK that's it. Camera stays in the box now till we reach the island.

LEFTERIS
You say you are a filmmaker but you do not want to shoot film. Strange.

DANIEL

Yannis just wants images and voiceover. He doesn't want a presenter. I can't use anything with you talking to the camera.

LEFTERIS

Yannis doesn't know about these things. Is it not better to have a friendly face than just images? Someone to make you feel welcome? A host?

DANIEL

It's cheesy. It's like 1970s style.

LEFTERIS

1970s cheese? You are wrong Daniel. It is not 1970s cheese.

EXT. FERRY. DAY

Brilliant blue sky and sea heated by a blazing Mediterranean summer sun.

DANIEL watches the churning foam. He turns back to the busy port of Piraeus receding. He descends into the hold.

INT. FERRY. DAY

DANIEL looks around. FAMILIES with BABIES, GERMAN TOURISTS, GREEK SAILORS. OLD MEN drinking coffee. LEFTERIS enters, looking for him.

LEFTERIS

What are you doing down here?

DANIEL

(stern) The camera stays in the box.

LEFTERIS

But this is the journey! This is the voyage. One minute of shooting.

DANIEL

Look we can call Yannis when we get to the island. You'll see he was very clear and specific in his instructions.

LEFTERIS

One minute. Just one minute.

DANIEL

(very stern) Absolutely not.

EXT. FERRY. DAY

LEFTERIS addresses the CAMERA held by a grudging DANIEL.

LEFTERIS

So here we are crossing the Aegean sea. Like Odysseus who wandered for ten years on the waves. Island to island he had to find the way back to Ithaca because the gods were angry with Odysseus. And all the men meanwhile were trying to get into the underwear of his wife Penelope.

DANIEL

(sarcastic) OK. Beautiful. Let's cut it there.

LEFTERIS

Historical background. Local colour. Do you not watch the Travel Channel?

LEFTERIS reaches across DANIEL and switches the CAMERA on again.

DANIEL

Hey!

LEFTERIS

The island was conquered by pirates, by the Turks by the Nazis. But through it all the Greeks remain stubborn as goats. Thanks be to God! Now the Germans and Angela Merkel try to conquer us again. Nothing doing, Angela! Of course German people are very welcome.

DANIEL

Good job. Outstanding.

LEFTERIS

You think so?

DANIEL

No, I do not think so. Jesus Christ.

EXT. SKYROS FERRY TERMINAL. DAY

The ferry docks. LEFTERIS and DANIEL gather belongings and get into LEFTERIS's CAR which chugs off. DANIEL stares out of the window.

EXT. SKYROS STREETS. DAY

The CAR halts in the narrow cobbled streets as PEOPLE block the way. LEFTERIS barks and remonstrates. DANIEL shifts impatiently.

LEFTERIS

Relax Daniel. Here on the island time slows down. Which is a great opportunity for more shooting. Take out the camera.

DANIEL
No! You hear me? No more shooting.

DANIEL has had enough. He grabs his bags and jumps out.

LEFTERIS
Where are you going?

DANIEL
See you up there.

DANIEL trudges up the hill.

EXT. SKYROS RESORT TERRACE. DAY

The terrace looks out over the hill to the sparkling sea beyond. A spectacular and tranquil outlook. DANIEL drops his bags and is still as the calming view washes over him.

Vines grow overhead and grapes hang down, olive trees sway on the slope.

Excitedly DANIEL unpacks the CAMERA and begins filming. The only sounds are a soft breeze, distant dog barking and some wind chimes.

DANIEL turns hearing footsteps and finds himself filming Californian ANNA (32) the most beautiful girl he has ever seen – barefoot in shorts and a bright vest.

ANNA smiles at him. DANIEL is transfixed and continues shooting. He zooms in on her. ANNA blows the camera a kiss and giggles.

DANIEL closes in. ANNA gets shy and turns away.

ANNA
(good humoured) Hey! Quit stalking me.

ANNA theatrically walks behind a bush. DANIEL turns off the camera.

DANIEL
Don't run away. I need you for scale.

ANNA
What?

DANIEL
I need you. As a foreground element to give human scale.

ANNA
That sounds sooo appealing. What do I get?

DANIEL
A lifetime supply of olive oil and ouzo. You know I can still see you.

ANNA
(laughing) Damn. You evil genius.

ANNA steps out from behind the bush. She smiles at DANIEL. They stand frozen – the electricity crackling between them. Finally ANNA moves along the terrace.

ANNA
OK then. Make it fast because right now I am in the zone.

DANIEL smiles and begins filming. He motions her to the edge of the terrace.

DANIEL
OK. Think serene. Think dawn of civilisation. Greek men talking philosophy. Plato. Socrates. Aristotle Onassis.

ANNA

How's this?

ANNA raises her arms and balances on one leg.

DANIEL

Awesome.

ANNA

'It was here long ago that mankind first encountered the chinchilla.'

DANIEL

(lowering the camera) What even is a chinchilla?

ANNA

A crepuscular rodent that lives in high altitude colonies.

DANIEL

What are you – a zoologist?

ANNA

I like exotic pets. Not really chinchillas. More like iguanas. What I really want is a Komodo dragon but that's totally illegal.

DANIEL

What do you have?

ANNA

A cat.

DANIEL

Exotic?

ANNA

Her behaviour is exotic. She's obsessed with my toes. Are we done?

DANIEL

Oh. Sorry.

DANIEL switches the CAMERA off. ANNA gently takes it from him.

**Nicholas Cohen** is a dual national US/UK writer/director educated at Cambridge and trained at the BBC Drama Directors Academy. He has directed Channel Four documentaries, BBC continuing drama series and feature films including *The Reeds* which After Dark/Lionsgate distributed theatrically in America. He hopes to shoot *First Person* next year.

# STEPHAN DRURY

## The Queue for Paradise

*A self-contained stage piece*

*Black stage. Spot on BRENDA, an old lady with a white topknot, holding a tin of baked beans. She has a cigarette in the other hand.*

BRENDA

For the first time in sixty-seven years I'm a winner. I mean, I actually gone and won something! Yeah, me. Only other time I ever come close I was six. Art competition. Drew a picture of the Queen. You know – to celebrate her coronation. Holding a glass of wine and a balloon she was. Very nice. A lovely bright blue. Came second. Though Miss Brown said I ought to have come first.

Anyway, horoscope in the local paper told me, 'The last few days have been a trial'. Days? Years more like. 'Last few days have been a trial, so tomorrow's surprise will feel like a new dawn. You may fear, but...' um, now what was it? Oh yeah, '...trust your heart.' Something like that. Or was it 'trust your gut'? I don't know – doesn't matter now though, does it?

*(BRENDA brandishes her beans)*

No. So I turns over the page, looking for the crossword, and bingo – there it was – in great big letters.

## Scene 2 (FLASHBACK)

*Stage is lit by an orange light – it is 4am in a supermarket car park in the urban wilds of the Essex border. Sprawled stage left is TIMON. He is a dishevelled reveller, comatose and still clutching the drink that felled him.*

*BRENDA enters. She looks about and queues next to TIMON. He is motionless and she barely notices him. BRENDA tightens her scarf and coat. BRENDA stares at TIMON. She turns away. TIMON snuffles and remains motionless. BRENDA does not react. She takes a can of hairspray out of her bag and touches up her hair.*

*MATT enters. He is wearing a woolly hat, three coats, a rucksack and is carrying a mattress. He struggles forward and notices BRENDA. BRENDA smiles. A beat.*

MATT

Shit.

*MATT joins the queue and plumps his mattress down. He ignores BRENDA.*

*MATT proceeds to set up camp. He sits on his mattress, pulls a blanket out of his rucksack, two bananas, a thermos flask, a large empty plastic bottle, two packets of soup and a Kindle. His kit neatly set out, MATT wraps himself in his blanket and begins to read his Kindle.*

*TIMON is motionless.*

BRENDA

Cold, isn't it?

MATT

Yep.

BRENDA

You're prepared.

MATT

Hmm-mm.

*A beat.*

BRENDA

Not normally out this early.

*MATT ignores her. He pours himself a drink out of the thermos and slurps it.*

BRENDA

But it's such an opportunity for someone. Do you think we need another supermarket? Mind you, they say Paradise is the cheapest there is. Cheaper than Aldi.

*MATT does not look at her. BRENDA turns away. MATT glances at BRENDA and pours another cup of coffee. He then removes a packet of laxatives, shakes a bag and empties it into the second cup. He stirs it with a flourish.*

MATT

*(without looking at BRENDA)*

Coffee?

BRENDA

What? Oh, that'd be nice. Not got any tea? Um... Yes – love one. Thanks.

*MATT hands BRENDA the poisoned cup. He watches her.*

BRENDA

Oh – it's hot. And strong. Just the thing though. Cheers.

*MATT grins. BRENDA struggles down her coffee. As she finishes, MATT chuckles. BRENDA looks at him.*

MATT

Sorry. Funny bit. In the book.

*MATT gestures for the cup, wipes it with some kitchen roll and slowly screws it back onto the thermos flask. He smiles as he turns back to his Kindle.*

*JANINE enters. She wears a high-cut, quilted jacket with the hood up. She looks about and joins the queue.*

JANINE

You all here for the opening?

BRENDA

Yes. And you?

JANINE

50% discount until midday? Abso-bloody-lutely! What you looking to get?

BRENDA

Not much.

JANINE

You're kidding, right? I got myself another card. Paradise do a store card too. Rate's crap. Still – I'm going wild.

*(to MATT)*

What about you?

*MATT ignores her. JANINE pulls a conspiratorial face to BRENDA. BRENDA looks away.*

JANINE

Cold, isn't it?

*MATT buries himself with his reading. BRENDA nods.*

JANINE

Hey – not got a spare cup for me, have you? No? Please yourself.

*(to BRENDA)*

So, what you here for then, if you're not bothered with anything?

BRENDA

The competition.

JANINE

What competition?

BRENDA

At the bottom of the ad.

JANINE

In the paper?

BRENDA

Yes. In the paper. At the bottom of the 50% discount offer.

JANINE

Really?

BRENDA

Yes.

JANINE

Truly?

BRENDA

Y es!

JANINE

What you win?

BRENDA

First one in Friday, Saturday, Sunday gets to pick one of the mystery golden envelopes.

JANINE

Real gold?

BRENDA
No.

JANINE

What's the prize?

BRENDA

Told you – it's a mystery. But it could be anything. A deluxe widescreen 3D TV or just a tin of beans.

*MATT is unsettled. He prepares himself a cup of soup.*

JANINE

Wow. Amazing. Heinz?

BRENDA

Maybe.

JANINE

I could do with a new TV. Old one's no good. Just 2D. And you know what kids are like. Always hassling me for the latest stuff. You after the TV, then?

BRENDA

I don't mind.

JANINE

I just want the discount. Still. The kids... Here, do you think you could let me—

*MATT and BRENDA dart JANINE a filthy look. MATT appears prone to violence.*

JANINE

Only asking. Christ. If you don't mind kids in poverty... Well you won't get it anyway.

*(Pointing at TIMON)*

He will.

*(TIMON is still motionless)*

Is he all right?

*BRENDA looks at TIMON. He is not moving. She taps him with her foot. No reaction.*

BRENDA

I think he's fine. Just asleep.

JANINE

You sure?

BRENDA

Yes.

JANINE

Checked his breathing, have you?

BRENDA

No.

JANINE

Well, you'd better. He might be sick. Choke on himself. I wouldn't want that on my conscience.

*BRENDA tentatively kneels down and listens.*

BRENDA

I think he's all right...

JANINE

Anything left in that bottle? I could use a drink.

*BRENDA starts to remove the bottle. TIMON groans and coughs up sick. He clutches the bottle. BRENDA jumps back. JANINE laughs.*

JANINE

Easy! Not dead then!

BRENDA

Disgusting.

JANINE

Yeah... and he's going to win. Hardly fair, is it? Bet he don't even know where he is. Or who he is. Give him a kick.

BRENDA

No.

JANINE

Phone him a taxi then.

BRENDA

No.

JANINE

Check his pockets. Bound to be an address and some cash. Go on. Fine. I'll do it.

*JANINE moves towards the front of the queue. MATT and BRENDA react as if under attack.*

JANINE

Easy! I'm not jumping the queue. Look – we've got to do something. He'll get hypothermia or whatever. You – mattress boy – help her shift him over there.

MATT

I'm not moving.

JANINE

You what?

MATT

He shouldn't have got so pissed.

JANINE

So you're going to let an old girl shift him? You bastard. Come on – what's your name?

BRENDA

Brenda.

JANINE

Brenda. I'm Janine. Let's shift him while this prick watches. Then you get to be first, don't you?

*JANINE and BRENDA drag TIMON over to one side. He steadfastly grips his drink. MATT quietly puts all his kit on the mattress. As BRENDA and JANINE are occupied he shifts his mattress to the front of the queue.*

JANINE

Eww – he reeks. Right – put him on his side so he ain't sick again.

*(backing away slightly)*

That's it... Now check his pockets for a wallet...

*BRENDA freezes. BRENDA and JANINE lock eyes. A beat. Suddenly both women dart for the queue. BRENDA, with a speed and fury that belies her age, grabs JANINE and pushes past her. JANINE falls over and BRENDA reaches the queue first. MATT has blocked her and is reading as if nothing had happened.*

JANINE

What is bloody wrong with you?

BRENDA

You tried to trick me!

JANINE

Oh shut up.

*MATT retrieves his large plastic bottle and conceals it under his blanket.*

BRENDA

I will not!

JANINE

Shut up.

BRENDA

You tried to take my place.

JANINE

Did not.

BRENDA

Did!

JANINE

Prove it.

BRENDA

Never in my life—

JANINE

Shut up.

BRENDA

People today.

JANINE

You pushed me over.

BRENDA

You cheated. And now he's first.

JANINE

You pushed me over – that's assault. I should… what is he doing?

*MATT has finished his secret urination into the bottle.*

*BRENDA looks uncomfortable and feels her belly.*

JANINE

You dirty bastard.

MATT

So?

JANINE

There's ladies present.

MATT

So?

JANINE

Unbelievable.

*A long beat. BRENDA looks increasingly uncomfortable.*

JANINE

You proud of yourself?

MATT

I don't care.

JANINE

Well, I do. You're gross.

MATT

If you've got to go, you've got to go.

JANINE

Not in front of me you don't. First her assaulting me and now you pissing in a bottle.

BRENDA glances at JANINE.

JANINE

What?

BRENDA

Nothing. I just...

JANINE

What then?

*JANINE plants her feet ready. She won't be moved. BRENDA looks at MATT. He stares back and smiles. A beat. BRENDA is in severe discomfort. Her gut grumbles.*

MATT

You all right?

BRENDA

Fine.

MATT

You sure?

BRENDA

Said I'm fine.

*MATT looks at his packet of laxatives and packs them lovingly into his rucksack. BRENDA is in pain. MATT smiles.*

MATT

Want me to hold your place?

BRENDA

No. Thank you.

MATT

Well, if you're not feeling—

BRENDA

I can manage.

*BRENDA is about to cry. Her body has failed her. JANINE looks at her. MATT winces and returns to his Kindle.*

JANINE

Is that you?

BRENDA ignores her and stares ahead.

JANINE

Jesus Christ, you stink.

*BRENDA fumbles in her pocket and pulls out her cigarettes and lighter. She is shaking as her lighter sparks but fails to light. The cigarette remains unlit and trembling in her mouth.*

JANINE

What is it with you people?

*JANINE positions herself further away. MATT is reading.*

BRENDA

Couldn't help it.

JANINE

Is this what happens when you get old? Christ. Why'd they let you out the home?

*MATT makes a show of coughing and waving away the smell. He rummages in his bag and pulls out ear plugs. MATT inserts them into his nose and returns to his Kindle.*

JANINE

It's like something gone and died.

BRENDA

It's not my fault.

*MATT glances at BRENDA and chuckles.*

JANINE

Oh, do us a favour!

BRENDA

If you can't stand the heat...

*JANINE puts her hood up and covers her mouth.*

JANINE

Should legalise euthanasia.

*BRENDA straightens her clothing. She takes out her can of hairspray, sprays her hair and tries to preen herself.*

JANINE

Don't think that will cover it.

*BRENDA is stoical and manages to light her cigarette. She glances at MATT and stares forward. A beat.*

*There is birdsong. A single warble followed by an answering chorus. MATT, BRENDA and JANINE listen.*

*MATT stands up and stretches.*

MATT

Morning, ladies!

*MATT hums as he starts to pack up his kit. BRENDA watches him. The mattress takes her eye.*

BRENDA

Nice mattress.

MATT

It is. Had it for years.

*BRENDA looks forward and takes a long drag. She takes out her hairspray, shakes it and gives it a squirt. Then, sparking her lighter, she lights the hairspray and unleashes a gout of flame. MATT screams.*

BLACKOUT.

**Stephan Drury** has worked in theatre for many years. Previous work includes: *Peppermint* (nominated for 'Best Film' and 'Best Screenplay' at the Southampton International Film Festival); *Megan and the Magpie* (Minotaur Radio); and an adaptation of *David Copperfield* (Mad Dogs & Englishmen Theatre Company). He is currently adapting *Don Quixote* for the stage and developing a TV comedy series for Silver Road Productions. For more information visit: www.stephandrury.wordpress.com

# ELIOT FALLOWS

## Dead Awkward

*A comedy short*

INT. SETH'S ROOM – NIGHT

SETH (20) lies asleep in bed. There's a scratch at the door. A creak of a floorboard. The door swings open. A shadow moves across the wall.

SETH

Hello?

Nothing for a moment. A voice from the darkness.

GEORGE

It's because we're thinking about it.

SETH

For pissing out loud.

GEORGE

We're making it stronger.

GEORGE (20) turns on the bedside lamp and sits on the end of the bed. He's wearing binoculars around his neck and holding an old library book: *Domestic Ghosts and Spirits.*

SETH

Last week, I asked you if you ate my cheese.

GEORGE
It survives off psychology and fear and emotion.

SETH
Because you have cheese on toast every Thursday and it was Thursday.

GEORGE
It was—

SETH
You told me it was the ghost.

GEORGE
That was a lie – that was – I had that cheese, but this one is real.

SETH
You have thirty seconds.

GEORGE
Every morning I notice my paperclip jar is on the other side of my desk. I put it on the right and it ends up on the left. How?

SETH
I don't know. Are you looking at it through a mirror?

GEORGE
No, it's a thing.

SETH
A thing.

GEORGE
A ghost thing.

SETH
Why would they move it?

GEORGE
To get attention?

SETH
You'd know all about that.

Seth turns off the lamp. George turns it back on and flips to a page in the middle of the book.

GEORGE
The book says the best way to weaken it is to ignore it.

SETH
You don't get course books, but you'll read that?

GEORGE
Because it thrives on us being scared.

Seth takes the book and drops it on the floor.

SETH
What do I have to do?

GEORGE
Nothing at all.

SETH
Nothing?

GEORGE
Yeah. It's best if we act like it's not there.

SETH

Get out.

Seth turns off the lamp.

INT. KITCHEN – DAY

Seth is listening to his headphones and frying some bacon. The smoke alarm screeches, he pulls out the headphones, takes the bacon off the hob and waves a magazine in front of the sensor until it stops.

When the house is quiet again, he notices the sound of the radio in the LIVING ROOM. White noise.

INT. LIVING ROOM – CONTINUOUS

Seth tiptoes towards the radio from the HALLWAY.

INT. HALLWAY – CONTINUOUS

Seth finds the *Domestic Ghosts and Spirits* book on the ground.

SETH

George?

Seth runs upstairs.

INT. GEORGE'S ROOM – CONTINUOUS

George is gone. Seth opens the pile of clothes and papers. He notices a tripod and camera pointing at the unmade bed.

INT. LIVING ROOM – DUSK

George enters, wearing his work polo and apron. Seth sits in the middle of the room with an empty chair in front of him.

SETH
Take a seat, George.

GEORGE
Seth—

SETH
Just take a seat.

George sits so the two men are facing each other. George moves his chair back slightly.

SETH (CONT'D)
This is because I love you.

GEORGE
Is this how desperate we are now? Are we doing this?

SETH
We have some stuff to talk about.

GEORGE
I'm all right with it, but I'm being the husband.

SETH
This is an intervention.

GEORGE
A what?

SETH
I know you've had some money problems before and you've got your job now, which is great, but if you're in some kind of trouble, you'll have to tell me before it goes too far.

GEORGE
Have we had a gas leak?

SETH
I found your camera.

GEORGE
My camera.

SETH
Set up to film your bed.

GEORGE
Right.

SETH
I know what you're doing, but it really isn't the best way to raise money George.

GEORGE
What am I doing, exactly?

SETH
I don't know the specifics obviously, without seeing it myself—

GEORGE
Seth—

SETH
Which I have no intention of doing. I know it seems fun now, but if something like this gets out, you'll never be able to get a job or get a girlfriend or anything.

GEORGE
Are you done?

Seth nods.

GEORGE (CONT'D)
I'm not filming myself having sex.

SETH
I know that, George.

GEORGE
I'm not filming myself wanking either.

SETH
Really?

GEORGE
It's for the ghost.

Seth lowers his head.

SETH
What?

INT. GEORGE'S ROOM – DUSK

George and Seth sit on George's bed. George is showing Seth the footage from the camera on his computer.

GEORGE
It's like *Paranormal Activity*. I film my room at night and the camera catches the ghost moving my paperclip jar.

SETH
You don't need that many paperclips. Not enough to warrant a jar.

The night-vision footage shows George asleep in bed.

GEORGE
The problem is, I film myself for eight hours and I don't have time to watch all of it back.

SETH
I kind of wish you were wanking now.

George looks at him.

SETH (CONT'D)
Not 'now'.
(points to screen)
Last night.

They continue to watch the screen.

SETH (CONT'D)
How long have you been doing this for?

GEORGE
Couple of weeks. Was that something?

George rewinds and presses play. They watch again.

SETH
No.

Seth looks around the room.

SETH (CONT'D)
Smells like old milk in here.

INT. LIVING ROOM – NIGHT

Seth lies on the sofa watching television. He turns it off and shuts his eyes for a moment. Something in the BATHROOM clatters on the ground. He opens his eyes.

INT. BATHROOM – CONTINUOUS

Seth slowly opens the door and turns on the light.

EXT. HOUSE – NIGHT

George arrives home and finds Seth sitting on the front step holding a vacuum cleaner, tears running down his face.

SETH

Can we move?

George sits by him and places a hand on his shoulder.

INT. LIVING ROOM – NIGHT

The two enter, Seth still holding the vacuum.

A creak from behind. Seth spins around and turns on the vacuum. There is nothing.

GEORGE

In the bathroom?

SETH

Yeah, on the mirror.

INT. BATHROOM – CONTINUOUS

George creeps in and stares at the mirror.

GEORGE

Huh.

Seth enters.

GEORGE (CONT'D)

What does that look like to you?

SETH
It looks like it's going to cut our hearts out.

On the mirror, drawn in what looks like blood is a love heart.

GEORGE
It looks like we've made a friend.

INT. LIVING ROOM – LATER

A makeshift Ouija board sits between George and Seth. A couple of tea lights on the table for atmosphere.

George places a finger on the cursor. He looks to Seth, who does the same.

SETH
This is stupid.

GEORGE
You're stupid with your hoover.

SETH
Sorry I'm not a ghost nerd.

GEORGE
A hoover.

George shakes his head and looks to the ceiling.

GEORGE (CONT'D)
Is anybody there?

A moment of nothing.

The cursor moves to YES.

GEORGE (CONT'D)
Good. What is your name?

The cursor moves again.

SETH
'Stacey'. It's a girl ghost.

GEORGE
Hi Stacey. I'm George.

They wave at nothing.

SETH
Seth.

GEORGE
Why are you here? Why this house?

The tea lights flutter a little. A soft, whispered voice flows through the room.

STACEY (OS)
I lived here. I died here.

Seth and George look at each other.

SETH
What room?

GEORGE
Yeah, what room?

STACEY (OS)
The room you are in.

Seth grimaces.

SETH

Gross.

George kicks him under the table.

GEORGE

Is there anything we can do? To help you move on I mean?

No response.

GEORGE (CONT'D)

Stacey?

STACEY (OS)

I've been watching you. For a year now.

SETH

Even in the shower?

STACEY (OS)

I was incomplete when I died. When I lived.

GEORGE

So what can we do?

No response again. The cursor begins to move on its own. Seth and George watch as it spells out a question:

Beat.

GEORGE (CONT'D)

'Will you go out with me?'

SETH

I'm going to bed.

GEORGE

Seth.

SETH
Is Derren Brown in the cupboard?

GEORGE
What?

Seth goes to the cupboard under the stairs and opens the door.

SETH
It's a hidden camera thing. A Derren Brown thing.

GEORGE
Derren Brown doesn't do pranks. That's Jeremy Beadle.

The cursor moves to the '?' symbol.

The lights flicker above them.

SETH
Yeah, wait a minute Stacey.

GEORGE
Seth, sit down.

Seth begrudgingly takes a seat again.

GEORGE (CONT'D)
Now, Stacey. Which one of us do you want to go out with?

SETH
Fuck me.

GEORGE
Stacey. We won't be offended. We just need to know.

The cursor moves to 'S'.

GEORGE (CONT'D)

S E T H.

Seth rolls his eyes.

SETH

Goddamn.

GEORGE

Really thought it'd be me. I'm well into magic and stuff.

STACEY (OS)

We were meant to be. I lie beside you at night and I will for eternity. Your hair like chestnut and your eyes like a pool of ice water.

SETH

Is this poetry?

STACEY (OS)

Do you like it?

Seth stands, looks George in the eye and moves to the door.

SETH

I'm going to bed.

He points to thin air.

SETH (CONT'D)

Don't follow me, Stacey.

George is left alone.

INT. GEORGE'S ROOM – NIGHT

Seth grabs the tripod and camera, clambering over the mess on the floor. He storms back out.

INT. SETH'S ROOM – CONTINUOUS

Seth sets up the tripod and camera to face his bed. He lies on top of the covers and stares at the ceiling.

INT. LIVING ROOM – NIGHT

George still at the Ouija board.

GEORGE
I'm kind of up for it if you want a rebound.

**Eliot Fallows** is a comedy writer, mostly working on television, video game and web series scripts. Although he does not currently have any professional credits, Eliot has made a fort out of the piles of scripts in his room.

# RUTH GAUKRODGER

## Planned Obsolescence

*An extract from a feature-length screenplay*

EXT. THE YORKSHIRE MOORS. DAY

The sun rises over the moors and illuminates the tracts of heather. A slow train edges over the horizon. It's a picture of tranquillity.

INT. TRAIN CARRIAGE THREE. DAY

CCTV cameras swivel on the ceiling of the train. A crowd of TOURISTS gather by the windows to look at the moors.

From the speakers:

PRISHA (OS)
The Yorkshire Moors Botanical Park spans over 1,750km. More than 80% of its plants are organic, making it an area of truly natural beauty.

There are some murmurs of appreciation from the tourists.

PRISHA (OS) (CONT'D)
The area was first awarded protected status in 2045, and now serves as home to many species of British flora and fauna.

INT. DRIVER'S CABIN. DAY

The cabin is crammed with screens showing live CCTV feeds. PETE (52, the driver) gazes out the window. Next to him, PRISHA (28, in oily overalls) hunches over the dashboard.

PRISHA

Turning up the birdsong in 4, 3, 2, 1.

Prisha pushes a lever.

EXT. THE YORKSHIRE MOORS. DAY

Hidden in a clump of heather is a speaker. It plays the dawn chorus.

INT. DRIVER'S CABIN. DAY

We hear the crescendo of the morning birdsong from outside.

PRISHA

Let's have some atmospheric fog.

Prisha flicks a switch and watches CCTV feed number 8.

CLOSE ON THE FEED: It shows a rock on the moors, which begins to pump out fog.

INT./ EXT. CARRIAGE THREE/ YORKSHIRE MOORS. DAY

The tourists watch as swirls of fog appear outside.

PRISHA (OS)

Wind, fog, rain and bright clear days are all
part of spring weather in the Botanical Park.

The tourists ogle the panoramic view.

INT. DRIVER'S CABIN. DAY

PRISHA

Today's foggy, because it's 40% more likely to prompt positive reviews and increase revenue.

Pete gives Prisha a disapproving look.

PRISHA (CONT'D)

Don't worry, the intercom's off. I've got a new effect. Watch this.

Prisha presses another button on the dashboard.

INT. CARRIAGE THREE. DAY

The carriage windows open. Small spouts on the window rims emit purple gas.

PRISHA (OS)

The wild heather of the moors has a famous floral smell. If you lean close to the windows, you may be able to make out the distinct but subtle fragrance.

The tourists crowd the open windows and inhale the air.

INT. DRIVER'S CABIN. DAY

PETE

Heather doesn't have a smell.

PRISHA

They don't know that.

Prisha gestures at the CCTV feed from carriage three. The tourists have their faces jammed up to the open windows.

PRISHA (CONT'D)
They love it. I'm a sensory artist, Pete. What can I say? The ends justify the means.

EXT. YORKSHIRE MOORS RAILWAY STATION. DAY

The train pulls into the station. A swarm of tourists alight and head towards a tourist office. A sign advertises prices:

FULL-DAY HIKING: £80,000.
HALF-DAY HIKING: £50,000.
CHILDREN HIKING: £30,000.

On the platform are three teenagers in school uniforms (CASSIUS, JOEL and DANIEL). Cassius is striking – he's large, tanned and has white blond hair. The boys board the train.

INT. DRIVER'S CABIN. DAY

Pete checks the dashboard of the train while Prisha swings in her chair.

PRISHA
That was probably my best performance yet.

PETE
I'm not sure. I think your enhancements may be damaging the authenticity of the tour.

A small screen next to the dashboard switches on and the face of a perky-looking man (ALEX, 30) appears.

ALEX
Good morning, Prisha! I hope today's tour went well.

PRISHA
What do you want, Alex?

ALEX

I couldn't help but notice that the feed from camera 6 is down. Please make sure you're regularly inspecting all train equipment. We need that CCTV feed back pronto.

Prisha gets out of her chair and picks up a toolbox.

ALEX (CONT'D)

Before you go, let's have a quick convo about last month's online reviews. Have you had a chance to look at them?

PRISHA

No. I try not to, as a rule.

ALEX

No matter. Let me read you some.

Prisha groans and resumes her seat.

ALEX (CONT'D)

This is from Paula Crag, age 46, review rating: 3 out of 10. 'Rubbish. The tour guide was adlibbing for most of the journey. At one point, she claimed that six species of wild bear inhabit the Yorkshire moors.'

PRISHA

Head Office told me that they were going to reintroduce them.

ALEX

'When I questioned her authority, she called me a lard-ass dunce.'

PRISHA

You hired me as a technician, not a tour guide.

ALEX

Government cuts mean we can't afford to hire both a guide and a technician. We all have to multitask. I'm overseeing five different local projects.

PRISHA

It's not my fault that tech training doesn't cover tour guide basics.

ALEX

How do you think you could have improved this woman's experience?

The train starts to move. Prisha stands, picks up her toolbox and gives Alex an exaggerated shrug.

PRISHA

Gee, Alex, I just don't know! Anyway, I should probably go and fix that camera.

ALEX

Please be polite to the general public – passengers and tourists alike. If you get any more negative reviews you'll be demoted.

Prisha leaves.

INT. TRAIN CARRIAGE THREE. DAY

Prisha looks up at the CCTV camera – a loose wire protrudes from its side. She mounts a seat, produces a wireless soldering iron and begins to fix the camera. She faces away from Joel, Daniel and Cassius, who sit further down the carriage. Joel and Daniel are absorbed in Cassius's spiel.

CASSIUS

In Tristan we had androids for everything.

You didn't even have to wipe your own arse.

JOEL

That sounds amazing.

CASSIUS

Most families had one to themselves. They were basically slaves.

Prisha's jaw clenches in irritation at the discussion.

DANIEL

I would love an android servant. Imagine never having to do your own homework again.

CASSIUS

I guess that's one use for them. We had sex droids. They lived in the red light district. Only £500 a pop.

Prisha's lost her patience. She turns to the boys.

PRISHA

You can't have sex androids. They're built with sex-drive inhibitors so perverts can't persuade them to have intercourse.

The boys look taken aback. They waver in their response.

JOEL

Wow, Cassius – she's calling you a pervert and a liar.

CASSIUS

There are overrides for the inhibitors. Twat.

PRISHA
No there aren't. The overrides are physically implanted.

Cassius eyes Prisha's overalls and her messy hair. Daniel and Joel grin – nervous and expectant.

CASSIUS
What makes you the expert?

PRISHA
Several years of training with the government's android production and improvement unit.

CASSIUS
I bet the government never told you about the overrides because they were worried you'd get distracted.

The boys laugh raucously. Prisha is unfazed.

PRISHA
There are no overrides. Even if there were, it's unlikely that androids would have a burning desire to sleep with an obese 16 year old.

JOEL
I think you hurt her feelings.

Joel and Daniel are still laughing – but Cassius isn't. The train comes to a stop.

CASSIUS
Come on, boys.

Cassius stands, takes out a phone from his pocket and begins to type. The teenagers exit the train.

INT. DRIVER'S CABIN. DAY

Alex is on screen, reading from a piece of paper. Prisha sits before him. Next to her, Pete monitors the train.

ALEX
'The engineer called me obese'. Rating: 0 out of 10.

PRISHA
Why do we let kids post reviews online? They undermine the system.

ALEX
It's a public forum, Prisha, you can't restrict who posts. You want to be a technician again? Now you are. You're being demoted to a local techie.

PRISHA
What? Come on, Alex. I'm really good at the tours. Don't make me work amongst the biomass again.

ALEX
Look at this as an opportunity for you to improve your people skills.

PRISHA
They don't need to be improved.

ALEX
There's a replacement technician boarding at the next station. You'll need to vacate the train there.

PRISHA
I thought we were friends, Alex.

Alex smirks.

ALEX

I'll make you a deal. If you can do just three local tech jobs in two days, and average a six star rating, you can come back to the train.

PRISHA

In two days? Easy.

ALEX

Your first job is at the boarding school. You'll have to change trains at the next station. Report back to me at the end of the assignment.

Alex's screen goes blank. He's gone for a moment and then returns.

ALEX (CONT'D)

Don't forget to reset Pete for the replacement technician.

Prisha kneels behind Pete and pushes a switch in the back of his chair. His eyes roll into his head and a red light shines from behind them. Prisha rolls up Pete's sleeve to reveal a barcode. She pulls out a scanner from her pocket and passes it over his arm. It beeps in recognition.

PRISHA

Reset droid 4382609.

Prisha switches Pete back on. He emits a low humming sound.

PRISHA
Sorry about that, Pete. Resets always seem kind of impolite.

**Ruth Gaukrodger**, 24, was born in Doncaster, South Yorkshire. She has a first class degree in Philosophy and English Literature, and writes stage and screenplays about philosophy, transhumanism and the environment.

# NICK HOPKINS

## Jumper

*A short film*

1. INT. *BLUE PETER* STUDIO – EVENING

1979. SIMON GROOM, *Blue Peter*-presenting legend, is talking to camera. Around him are children's paintings on easels.

SIMON GROOM

But the one that really caught our eye was this brilliant painting of Doctor Who battling the Daleks.

The camera focuses on a pretty good painting of Tom Baker facing off against some Daleks.

SIMON GROOM (CONT'D)

You might have guessed the artist is a bit of a *Doctor Who* fan but, if there's any doubt, here's a photo of him in all his Time Lord finery.

A monitor flicks to a Polaroid photograph of a young boy in a huge, unwieldy home-knitted scarf and a too-large-for-him floppy brown hat.

SIMON GROOM (CONT'D)

So congratulations Eliot Chalker, aged 11. A well deserved *Blue Peter* badge is on its way to you.

2. INT. LIVING ROOM – CONTINUOUS

ELIOT CHALKER sits motionless, cross-legged on the floor, a piece of toast and jam in his hand, frozen midway to his mouth. He is transfixed and horrified by what he's watching.

SIMON GROOM
(on the TV, chuckling)
Let's have a look at that marvellous costume again, shall we?

The TV again switches to the photo of ELIOT as The Doctor.

Back to ELIOT, still unable to move. The sound from the TV drains away. Time slows.

ADULT ELIOT (VO)
A painting of mine. On national television. Sent in by my mother without my knowledge. Along with the photo. I was outed. I was a *Doctor Who* fan.

Time returns to normal. ELIOT drops his toast.

3. EXT. SCHOOL PLAYGROUND – MORNING

Quick cut. A busy playground. ELIOT stands alone. A ball hits him smack in the side of the head. KIDS laugh.

SCHOOL KID 1
Spanner!

EXT. SCHOOL PLAYING FIELD – DAY

ELIOT is tackled to the ground by a grinning TALL KID.

TALL KID
Knobhead.

4. INT. SCHOOL CANTEEN – DAY

A GIRL flicks a pea from her plate; it hits ELIOT in the eye.

GIRL

Fucking Joey.

5. INT. SCHOOL CORRIDOR – DAY

ELIOT walks down the corridor.

ADULT ELIOT (VO)

I was always led to believe only spanners, knobheads and Joeys like me watched *Blue Peter*, but it seemed the entire world had seen me and my scarf that previous evening.

Ahead of him appear a GANG of FIVE KIDS.

GANG LEADER

There he is.

SPOTTY KID

Oi flid, where's your TARDIS now?

FAT KID

Bundle!

The KIDS race towards ELIOT in slow motion. ELIOT stands facing them, too frightened to run.

ADULT ELIOT (VO)

Kids these days don't know how lucky they are. Back then a lad coming to school in pigtails and a dress was safer than being known as a *Doctor Who* nerd.

In slow motion the boys leap as one at the terrified ELIOT, who is taken down as if by a pack of starving hyenas. They descend towards the floor, ELIOT hitting the ground first, his mouth opens wide as the air in his lungs is pushed out under the weight of his attackers.

Time returns to normal and the gang pummel and jump on ELIOT till the GANG LEADER pulls them off.

GANG LEADER

Shit.

He pulls back ELIOT's blazer to reveal blood and gore splashed across his shirt. They all stop for a moment then the SPOTTY KID reaches into ELIOT's blazer inside pocket and pulls out a squashed jam sandwich which has squeezed its contents from within the cling film wrapping.

SPOTTY KID

You bender.

The SPOTTY KID drops the sticky remains in ELIOT's face. ELIOT lies there, resigned to his fate.

Pull out and fade.

6. EXT. RAILWAY BRIDGE. LEDGE – DAY

Present day. A railway line snakes through beautiful countryside. A vast Victorian brick bridge stands a dizzying height above a fast moving river. ELIOT, now mid-forties, sits watching the view, leaning against the crumbling bricks, his legs dangling over the ledge. From where he is he can't be seen from the line side. He's wearing a *Blue Peter* badge.

ELIOT

(to camera)

Now, that experience taught me the only thing

I ever really took away from school. Never be yourself. Never expose what you really think or who you really are. That painting on *Blue Peter* was probably the only honest artistic work of my life. Now, I admit, things may not have turned out exactly like I'm painting them – excuse the pun – but I haven't spent a life on the streets or sought succour in alcohol. I have actually been very successful. In a way. And from painting. But what's my legacy? Watercolours of bloody steam trains. Endless postcards of supposedly cute, fluffy animals. And my greatest triumph? The cover of a shortbread box which sells by the million the world over.

He reaches into his jacket and takes out a jam sandwich wrapped in cling film. He unwraps it and eats, taking in the spectacular view.

ELIOT
(to camera) (CONT'D)
That shortbread box. You'll have seen it. Twat in a kilt with a West Highland terrier next to him, packet of Glen Hambledon shortbread sticking out his sporran. Ghastly. Bought me a house with a pool, that. Fucking hate shortbread though.

A noise behind him makes him turn to see a woman in her early 20s clamber over the rail side wall and drop down to the ledge. She spots him and they regard each other awkwardly.

ELIOT

Hello.

RUTH

Hi...

RUTH stands self-consciously. She points to the ledge.

RUTH

Do you mind?

ELIOT

Not at all.

They are about ten feet away from each other, but there's at least a hundred feet either side of them.

RUTH

If you need some space..?

ELIOT

It's OK.

RUTH sits, her legs also dangling over the edge. They both look out across the countryside.

ELIOT (CONT'D)

It's a lovely day.

RUTH

Yeah...

A long silence.

ELIOT

Are you from around here?

RUTH

Here and there.

ELIOT

That's a nice necklace. It suits you. Matches your eyes.

RUTH doesn't know what to say to that, so she turns to look back at the view.

ELIOT
(aside, to camera)
You've come up here to commit suicide, a final desperate act of artistic emancipation and you're chatting up some woman?! What's the matter with you?

He discreetly looks over to her legs.

ELIOT
(to himself)
Great legs though.

RUTH
I'm sorry?

ELIOT didn't realise he'd said that aloud.

ELIOT
The ledge... It's... great.

RUTH is puzzled and looks at the ledge.

ELIOT (CONT'D)
... The brickwork...

He tails off and looks back out across the view for a few moments before turning back to her.

ELIOT (CONT'D)
No, you know what, I wasn't talking about the ledge. I think, in whatever time I have left I should just cut the bullshit. I said, you have great legs.

Another silence while they both process that. She looks down at her legs.

RUTH

You like them?

ELIOT

Yes.

RUTH

Huh.

(a pause)

Strange place to try and pick someone up.

ELIOT

I wasn't trying to pick you up.

RUTH

Oh.

ELIOT looks puzzled.

ELIOT

Did you want me to?

RUTH

No.

ELIOT

It's just you seem disappointed. That I wasn't trying to pick you up.

RUTH shrugs.

ELIOT (CONT'D)

I mean, if I was in a bar or something, I'd definitely want to.

Silence again.

RUTH

In whatever time you have left? Are you going

to die soon or something?

ELIOT looks down at the drop to the river.

ELIOT

Well...

RUTH

You're not a jumper?

ELIOT

Course I am.

She points to the second sandwich, still wrapped up on the ledge.

RUTH

Who brings a sandwich to a suicide? Worried you might get hungry on the way down?

ELIOT

I'm eating a jam sandwich because jam sandwiches remind me of a certain time in my life.

RUTH

Like Proust and his madeleines?

ELIOT

I don't know... what that means.

RUTH

How can you have an appetite at a time like this?

ELIOT

(pointedly)

You know just now you asked if I wanted some space?

RUTH shrugs.

RUTH
So what brings you here?

ELIOT
A lot of things.

She looks at his left hand; there's a tan mark on his ring finger.

RUTH
Ah, divorce.

ELIOT
Amongst others.

RUTH
34% of marriages end in divorce before the 20th anniversary.

ELIOT
And?

RUTH
I don't see any of them up here. You're divorced, you're unhappy. Just sounds like one of your lines in that pick-up bar.

ELIOT
For starters, that was a hypothetical pick-up bar, but... I'm in my mid-forties, I'm unhappy, unfulfilled...

RUTH
'I Can't Get No Satisfaction.' I don't believe Mick Jagger when he says that either but at least it's a good tune. So. Are you some kind of failure?

ELIOT
Artistically, I think so.

RUTH
Only people with no real problems
say that. You're not broke? Or destitute?

ELIOT
Well, no...

RUTH looks at him.

ELIOT (CONT'D)
But I hate what I do. I'm a sell-out. I paint crap.

RUTH
Do they pay you for it?

ELIOT
Yeah, but...

He tails off again.

RUTH
How many paintings have you sold?

ELIOT
I don't know. Hundreds.

RUTH
Van Gogh sold two.

ELIOT
People always say that. Bloody Van Gogh. At least they were two good ones!

RUTH
Bloke jumped off here a few years ago, hit the water so hard his head flew off.

ELIOT
Jesus!

RUTH
They found it six weeks after the rest of him.

ELIOT
Do you mind?

RUTH
Aren't you worried about who you're leaving behind?

ELIOT
Nope.

RUTH stands up.

RUTH
Let's go together.

ELIOT
What?!

She shuffles over to him.

RUTH
Let's jump.

She goes to pull him up, almost sending him over.

ELIOT
If you push me, it's technically murder, you know?

RUTH
(impatient)
If we're going, let's go. Come on.

ELIOT
I didn't realise there was a rush. Or a 'we.'

Despite himself ELIOT gets up. They pause.

ELIOT (CONT'D)
Isn't this going to seem weird? The two of us? People'll assume it was some lovers' death pact or something.

RUTH
That's romantic.

ELIOT
Yes, but we've never... I don't know anything about you.

RUTH
Worried I might damage your reputation?

ELIOT
No, but...

RUTH
Neither you, your jam sandwiches nor your expensive watch are going anywhere but home today.

She scrabbles back up the wall, then turns back to face him.

RUTH (CONT'D)
You know, really Eliot, it seems to me you just need to be less of a knobhead.

She disappears onto the track side. ELIOT stands puzzled for a second then grabs his remaining sandwich, stuffs it in his inside pocket and jumps over the wall.

7. EXT. RAILWAY BRIDGE. TRACK – DAY

He drops down onto the track side. The bridge and track lie straight for hundreds of yards either side. No sign of RUTH. He looks down at his shirt. In climbing the wall his jam sandwich has squished through his jacket pocket.

RUTH (OC)

Boo!

ELIOT jumps and turns to see RUTH poke her head from behind a junction box by the bridge wall. He looks faintly disappointed.

RUTH (CONT'D)

Aw, did you think I was an angel or something? Sent to rescue you?

ELIOT

No...

RUTH

Spanner. Thanks for the compliment on my legs by the way. People always say it's what's on the inside that counts. That's partly true, but the outside's important too. That's the bit that entices you in.

She takes something out of her pocket and chucks it at him. He catches it. It's a packet of Glen Hambledon shortbread with Eliot's illustration on the front.

He looks up. Ruth has gone again. He looks behind the box. He looks up and down the track. Impossibly, she's nowhere to be seen.

He looks at the packet, opens it and takes out a piece of shortbread. He pops it in his mouth, crunches it cautiously and nods.

ELIOT

Not so bad after all.

Eliot walks down the track.

THE END

**Nick Hopkins** came to UEA after seventeen years in the film and television industry. For much of that time he was an assistant director on numerous films and TV shows. Subsequently, he has written three episodes of the BBC drama *New Tricks* and currently has a series in development.

# MONTE JACKSON

## Tourner

*A play in one act*

SCENE 1

Two train seats on opposite sides of the front of the stage, both in slightly battered condition. The remaining area of the stage, including the area between the seats, is dark. In the seat on the stage-left side of the stage, is ADRIAN DAHL, a German, aged thirty-nine. He is tall and slender, with a wan but handsome face and a nervous demeanour. He is dressed in blacks and greys, with a dark overcoat and gloves. Next to his seat is a heavy-looking suitcase. In the opposite seat is OLIVER LENNOX, a Scotsman, aged forty-two. He is slightly shorter than ADRIAN, and of medium build. OLIVER appears confident and composed in a tailored brown suit and overcoat with a scarf. Next to his seat is a medium-sized attaché case. With the faint sound of a train running on tracks in the background, OLIVER reaches into the pocket of his coat and draws out a letter. On the other side, ADRIAN looks out a window – he is troubled. Unfolding the letter, OLIVER begins reading it aloud.

OLIVER LENNOX: My dearest Oliver, I do hope this letter reaches you in time. As I mentioned in my last letter,

Leaning his head back against his seat and closing his eyes, ADRIAN joins in, reciting the letter as OLIVER reads it.

OLIVER/ADRIAN: I am going to Paris – for good this time. I take the train from Berlin on Friday and have arranged for my things to have arrived by Wednesday.

ADRIAN trails off again and falls silent while OLIVER continues reading.

OLIVER LENNOX: If you are, by chance, in the area, I was hoping that you would agree to meet me one afternoon.

ADRIAN laughs nervously.

I was thinking we could meet at the café on the corner near your old flat – the one where I almost turned your coffee over into your lap and had to leave because I was too mortified to just buy you a new cup.

OLIVER shakes his head fondly.

I'm sure that you know the place, I'm just

being ridiculous about it. Yours as always,

OLIVER trails off, taking his eyes off the letter for the first time, and ADRIAN finishes the letter.

ADRIAN DAHL: Adrian.

Leaning on his armrest, ADRIAN returns his gaze to the window, and OLIVER carefully folds the letter, but does not replace it.

Black out.

SCENE 2

The outdoor dining area of a Paris café in 1949, late afternoon. At a secluded table in a corner is OLIVER, still in a brown tailored suit, but without his overcoat and scarf. He is reading a paperback novel and smoking, a coffee sitting in front of him, largely ignored. The seat across from him is saved with a spread newspaper and his attaché case sits near his feet. A small span of time passes, and then ADRIAN enters, staying a fair distance from the table at first. He is wearing the same colour scheme as before, but with a scarf. He still wears the gloves from the previous scene. It takes him longer than he would like, but he finally spots OLIVER, who does not notice him at first. He does not immediately approach the table, instead pacing back and forth and suffering several false starts before he finally seems to decide to go for it. As ADRIAN steels himself for the approach, OLIVER notices him. The two make eye contact, and OLIVER closes his book and pointedly stubs his cigarette out in his saucer. Resolute, ADRIAN makes a beeline for OLIVER's table, but almost knocks over another table. He sheepishly rights it before continuing. Once he makes it to the table, ADRIAN pauses to reassure himself.

OLIVER LENNOX: No, it's me.

ADRIAN relaxes, pulling his gloves off hastily.

ADRIAN DAHL: Oliver!

Laying his gloves on the table, he sits down, heedless of the newspaper, and takes OLIVER's hand as if eager to confirm that he is real.

OLIVER seems charmed.

OLIVER LENNOX: Good to see you, Adrian.

ADRIAN looks at OLIVER for a long time, as if marvelling that he is actually there.

OLIVER pulls another cigarette from his pack, lights up, and gives ADRIAN a quick, suave once-over.

You haven't changed much. (beat) You look good.

ADRIAN DAHL: (flustered) You haven't changed at all.

OLIVER LENNOX: Is that a good thing or a bad thing then?

There is an awkward moment in which ADRIAN appears unsure as to how to answer the question. Stalling, ADRIAN takes one of OLIVER's cigarettes and lights it.

Didn't know you smoked.

ADRIAN DAHL: Maybe some things do change.

OLIVER seems thrown off. He picks up his coffee cup and takes a sip from it. It is cold.

Noticing, ADRIAN starts as if to go and find a waiter, but OLIVER stops him.

OLIVER LENNOX: It's fine. (beat) I take it you're settling in all right?

ADRIAN DAHL: It's been a long process. I'm sure you know how these things can be.

OLIVER touches the top of ADRIAN's hand.

OLIVER LENNOX: Well you're here now, that's what matters.

ADRIAN is surprised by the gesture, but pleased despite himself.

ADRIAN DAHL: I'm... I'm glad you came. Really, I am.

OLIVER seems to disregard the obvious affection, and ADRIAN becomes wary again.

OLIVER LENNOX: So, why Paris?

ADRIAN shrugs.

ADRIAN DAHL: There's nothing for me back in Berlin.

OLIVER LENNOX: Isn't your sister there?

ADRIAN DAHL: (dry) Klara is married now – quite happily, I might add, in West Berlin.

OLIVER looks surprised despite struggling to conceal his reaction.

ADRIAN DAHL: Berlin isn't for me, not any more. Too many bad memories.

OLIVER LENNOX: I'd hardly call Paris a blank slate.

ADRIAN DAHL: There's more good than bad.

OLIVER LENNOX: Four years of being stationed in an occupied country—

ADRIAN DAHL: (quietly) Five years.

OLIVER LENNOX: Five years of being stationed in an occupied

country by a government you didn't even believe in! (beat) Look, Adrian, I know that Germany isn't exactly home any more – I can't imagine it would be, but you can hardly pretend that—

ADRIAN DAHL: I think I've earned the right to 'pretend' anything I want, Oliver.

ADRIAN stubs out his cigarette in the saucer, next to OLIVER's first.

Wouldn't you say?

OLIVER laughs, but it feels forced.

OLIVER LENNOX: I might. Might not. Depends on the place, I suppose.

ADRIAN seems to think something over, coming to a swift conclusion.

ADRIAN DAHL: Do you want to see it?

OLIVER LENNOX: What?

ADRIAN DAHL: Where I live. It's all settled now.

OLIVER LENNOX: Oh! The new flat! (suddenly coy) Well, if you're inviting me.

ADRIAN is unimpressed.

OLIVER laughs, putting out his cigarette and tucking the paperback into his attaché.

Of course.

ADRIAN gets up first and almost puts his gloves on, but then stops and offers his hand and, grinning, OLIVER takes it.

EXIT ADRIAN and OLIVER.

SCENE 3

ADRIAN's flat, evening of the same day.

The flat is minimalist but comfortable, with simple, pragmatic furnishings. There is a small coffee table and a sofa, both of which are dotted with books.

There are doorways on the stage-right and left sides of the room, leading into the kitchen and bedroom. In one corner is a coatrack.

ADRIAN and OLIVER enter, both of them intoxicated, though ADRIAN appears to be slightly more so than OLIVER and is leaning a little on the other's shoulder. Both men seem relaxed in each other's company – a shift from the previous scenes.

ADRIAN DAHL: No, really Oli, you didn't need to pay for dinner.

OLIVER laughs and pulls ADRIAN closer to him.

OLIVER LENNOX: Please, it was the least I could do.

ADRIAN starts to protest, and OLIVER stops him with a peck on the lips.

Call it a housewarming gift.

He kisses him again, and any tension left in ADRIAN's posture melts away.

ADRIAN DAHL: And what would you call this?

OLIVER LENNOX: (flirtatious) Oh this? This is for old times' sake.

OLIVER drops onto the sofa and clumsily manoeuvres ADRIAN down into his lap.

You really are lovely, aren't you?

ADRIAN looks at him wonderingly, letting his hands wander over OLIVER's face, neck and shoulders as if reacquainting himself with the contours of his features before settling against OLIVER's chest.

ADRIAN DAHL: No I'm not.

OLIVER's demeanour, while still drunk, is suddenly very tender, and he seems less intent on seducing ADRIAN and more on convincing him of his sincerity.

This consists of both tender gestures from OLIVER, which are received by ADRIAN with varying degrees of receptiveness, and attempts at kissing him, which are almost always thwarted.

Eventually, ADRIAN buries his face in OLIVER's neck.

OLIVER LENNOX: I've missed you so.

ADRIAN mumbles into OLIVER's neck.

ADRIAN DAHL: I wish I could believe that.

OLIVER LENNOX: What was that?

ADRIAN doesn't reply.

OLIVER tips ADRIAN's chin up and moves to kiss him again, but ADRIAN pulls away, angry.

ADRIAN DAHL: Oliver.

OLIVER LENNOX: (playful) Adrian.

OLIVER pulls ADRIAN back against him and tries once more to kiss him, but ADRIAN pushes himself backwards and scrambles to his feet.

ADRIAN DAHL: Oliver, stop it.

OLIVER is shocked and uncertain of what exactly he has done wrong.

OLIVER LENNOX: Adrian? What on earth?

OLIVER stands. ADRIAN takes a step back.

ADRIAN DAHL: You're drunk.

OLIVER is confused by the accusation – of course he is. They both are.

OLIVER LENNOX: So are you. We've both been drinking, love.

He reaches for ADRIAN's hand.

I don't get what the big deal is, Adrian.

ADRIAN snatches his hand away.

ADRIAN DAHL: I said stop it.

OLIVER stares at him, still stunned and a little hurt, but then frustrated by the sudden change in ADRIAN, he gives up.

OLIVER LENNOX: Fine. Tell you what. I'm going to shower and—

ADRIAN DAHL: Good. Sober yourself up.

OLIVER gives him a 'And what about you?' look, but continues.

OLIVER LENNOX: And then we can talk this over.

He waits for ADRIAN to respond, and when he fails to receive a response, he EXITS through the bedroom. Offstage, there is the sound of a shower running.

ADRIAN paces anxiously, his entire form radiating tension, but after a moment, he EXITS into the bedroom.

**Monte Jackson**'s lifelong affair with writing for the stage began in childhood through the influence of growing up in a theatre production company. While an undergraduate, he has written three plays, including his honours thesis entitled *The Gospel of Judas,* which he also directed as a reader's theatre production.

# HARRY MASON

## Personal Space

*A short film script*

INT. SHOPPING CENTRE – EVENING

HUNDREDS OF SHOPPERS pour through a packed centre. Tinsel and flashing lights hang from every possible surface. Cliff Richard and Shakin' Stevens blare out. An animatronic Santa waves eerily from a nativity display.

People barge around in a frenzy, armed with bag upon bag of shopping, sharp elbows and aggressive glares.

INT. COFFEE SHOP – CONTINUOUS

Ducking away from this into a plush coffee shop is ALFIE (19), 6 feet 5 inches of gangly awkwardness. He tries to recover himself.

INT. COFFEE SHOP – LATER

Alfie reaches the till. It's manned by LAURA (20), pretty despite her coffee-spattered uniform and antler ears.

LAURA

Hello!

Alfie thrusts a sandwich and bottle of water on the counter.

ALFIE
These. Please.

LAURA
Did you want your panini heated up?

ALFIE
No please. (frowns) Thank you.

LAURA
All righty, that'll be—

A GAGGLE OF MIDDLE-AGED LADIES flutter past. Alfie practically leaps forward to avoid them.

LAURA (CONT'D)
—er, £2.40 please.

Laura puts her hand out. Alfie swerves around it and puts a collection of coins and coppers on the counter.

ALFIE
It's the right amount, I counted it. Three times.

LAURA
Guess I'll take your word for it!

She laughs and scoops up the money. Alfie simply walks away.

INT. COFFEE SHOP – LATER

At a table, Alfie places his sandwich down (one bite left uneaten) and brushes the crumbs into a napkin.

Laura watches him scrawl in a jotter as she collects empty mugs.

ALFIE
(muttered) Debenhams. Marks and Spencer.

Thorntons?

He scribbles something out. Laura watches on, intrigued.

INT. SHOPPING CENTRE – EVENING

Alfie braves the crowds but is unable to stop himself twitching.

People press in from every angle; even when Alfie veers away from one person he finds himself closer to another. His breathing is rapid and jagged.

The crowds suddenly part. Up ahead, a tiny girl – ESMÉ (5) – is charging forward hell for leather.

She slams straight into Alfie. Stunned silence. Alfie lets out a frustrated howl. Everyone stops and stares. Alfie glances around, embarrassed, before hurrying away.

INT. DEBENHAMS – EVENING

Alfie speeds down an aisle. He stops by some perfume but clearly doesn't know where to begin. He picks one bottle up and stares at it. He squeezes it but jumps back at the spray. He sniffs, then scrunches his nose.

Just around the corner of the aisle, Esmé appears. She tiptoes forward, sticking her head around to watch Alfie.

Alfie stops. Peering down, he notices Esmé. She scampers away, giggling.

INT. DEBENHAMS – LATER

Alfie blusters hopelessly through piles of blouses.

His head cocks to the side – Esmé's head is peeping out from a clothing rack. She quickly retreats. Alfie darts away.

INT. DEBENHAMS – LATER

Alfie rides the escalator upwards.

On the adjacent downwards escalator appears Esmé. She ducks down mischievously as she passes Alfie. He is unnerved, and watches her in bewilderment as he is carried up and away.

INT. DEBENHAMS – LATER

Alfie stalks along. Esmé appears from nowhere and sidles up to him as if they were the oldest of friends.

ESMÉ

Hiya!

Alfie jumps out of his skin.

ALFIE

What do you want?

Esmé reaches for his hand. He yanks it back and bolts ahead but Esmé simply follows along, little legs straining to keep up.

ESMÉ

Do you want to be my friend?

ALFIE

No.

ESMÉ

I've got lots of friends. Ruby, Ella, Dexter... (frowns) he's a boy and smells bad. Hannah isn't my best friend because she stole my pencil case.

Alfie doesn't respond.

ESMÉ (CONT'D)
Will you be my best friend?

ALFIE
I don't want a friend.

ESMÉ
Oh.

She shrugs and skips along.

ESMÉ (CONT'D)
What are you doing?

ALFIE
I need to find a Christmas present. I'd like you to leave me alone.

ESMÉ
You don't want a friend?

ALFIE
I said that. Twice.

ESMÉ
But everybody wants a friend! Read Winnie the Pooh, he'll explain it to you.

Alfie stops, unable to make any sense of Esmé.

ALFIE
Don't you have a mum with you?

ESMÉ
Nope, I'm all by myself!

Alfie shakes his head and carries onwards. Esmé's face lights up.

ESMÉ (CONT'D)
Does this mean we're friends?

ALFIE
Just... stop standing so close.

He steps to the side.

ALFIE (CONT'D)
This far. Two feet. At all times.

Esmé steps nearer – Alfie takes one step back. She retreats – he steps forward again. Alfie nods and they walk on.

INT. DEBENHAMS – LATER

Alfie studies a collection of garish figurines. Esmé stands two feet behind.

ESMÉ
So, Alfred?

ALFIE
No. Just Alfie.

ESMÉ
Like the frog on telly?

ALFIE
I don't know.

Esmé inches a finger towards Alfie. At a precise point, his entire frame tenses. She stops and pulls her finger back.

INT. DEBENHAMS – LATER

The mismatched pair stride along, Esmé chatting incessantly.

ESMÉ

...and then he goes through the woods, and then he gets to Grandma's house and says 'I'll huff and I'll puff and—'... no, that's not right...

Alfie grimaces and puts his hands over his ears. Just then, the overhead Tannoy system clicks on.

TANNOY

(bored) Attention please, attention. A young girl has been separated from her family. Name: Esmé Roberts. Age: 5.

The preoccupied shoppers pay the message little attention. Alfie remains oblivious as Esmé prances around him.

TANNOY (CONT'D)

Esmé is of African origin, 3 foot tall, dark hair in pigtails, wearing a pink jumper and a small purple rucksack. Last seen near H&M.

Alfie lets his hands down and heads out, Esmé in tow.

TANNOY (CONT'D)

Anyone with information is asked to report to security on the upper shopping level. That is all.

INT. SHOPPING CENTRE – EVENING

Alfie and Esmé march through the crowds, their two-feet gap somehow remaining intact.

ESMÉ

But how can you not like people?

ALFIE

They scare me.

ESMÉ

You're weird.

No reaction.

ESMÉ (CONT'D)

What do you like? I like green, and sandwiches with no crusts, and the night garden off of *In the Night Garden*.

ALFIE

I like numbers.

ESMÉ

Sums? Urgh!

ALFIE

Lists.

ESMÉ

I sent my list to Father Christmas!

ALFIE

And Walter Strauss's theory of universal stability.

Esmé scrunches her face.

ESMÉ

You *are* weird.

INT. PEACOCKS – EVENING

Alfie attempts to locate the price tag on a T-shirt as Esmé clambers into the depths of a clothing rack.

ESMÉ (OOV)
(from within) Alfie! Alfie! Watch me!

Two ELDERLY LADIES pass the rack. The sleeve of a jumper waves at them.

ESMÉ (OOV) (CONT'D)
Pick me! Pick meee!!!

The ladies gasp. A faint smile flickers around Alfie's mouth.

INT. HMV – EVENING

Esmé yawns as Alfie flicks through DVDs. The gap between them seems to have narrowed.

ESMÉ
Who's the present for?

ALFIE
My mum. For Christmas.

ESMÉ
But you're a grown-up!

ALFIE
I need to find her a nice present. Last week she said 'After this crapper of a year, Christmas with just the two of us might finally be an opportunity for something good.' That's exactly what she said, so I saved £20 especially. Now I have to get her a nice present or Christmas won't be something

good, we won't have a good day and her crapper of a year will just ge t worse.

Esmé has completely lost track of what Alfie is saying. She blinks.

ESMÉ

I like pick-and-mix. We should get pick-and-mix.

INT. CLINTONS – EVENING

Esmé sneaks behind a BUSINESSMAN queuing at the till. Alfie watches from the doors, knuckles in his mouth.

Esmé taps the businessman on the back. As he turns, she scoots sideways so he cannot see her. He shakes his head and turns back.

Esmé taps him on the other side. He turns again, faster this time, but still sees no one.

Esmé waits, suppressing giggles. She then raps him hard on the back. He spins around and she bolts away in hysterics. Alfie dashes after Esmé, unable to stop himself laughing.

INT. SHOPPING CENTRE – EVENING

The pair regain their breaths. They now stand even closer to each other.

ESMÉ'S MOTHER (OS)

There she is!

Alfie and Esmé wheel round. ESMÉ'S MOTHER, a buxom woman in bright African prints, stands across the concourse surrounded by concerned family members. She points at them. Before Alfie can even look down, Esmé has peeled away and thunders down an escalator.

Alfie runs after her, trying hopelessly to avoid contact with other shoppers. Esmé's family follow, shouting and hollering.

INT. SHOPPING CENTRE. LOWER FLOOR – CONTINUOUS

Esmé zigzags along but Alfie is hot on her heels, knocking bags from indignant shoppers' hands as he goes. Esmé's family fall behind.

Alfie rounds a corner and almost rips over Esmé – she stands stone still, face pressed against the window of Wilkinson's.

ALFIE
What are you doing?

Esmé pretends not to hear him. She gazes at a hand-held hoover.

ALFIE (CONT'D)
That was your mum, wasn't it?

No response.

ALFIE (CONT'D)
That's it, you have to go back right away or we'll both get into a lot of trouble! (beat) What are you looking at?

ESMÉ
It's beautiful!

Alfie notes other children flooding into the Disney store opposite. He groans.

Laura then appears behind them. Her eyes brighten, as if happy to see Alfie and Esmé.

She watches them enter Wilkinson's. Other shoppers grumble as they push past, but Laura is transfixed by what she sees.

Alfie and Esmé stand at the till. A server scans the hoover. Alfie pulls out £20 and, after a moment's hesitation, places it on the counter. He hands the hoover to a gleeful Esmé.

Laura smiles.

Alfie makes to leave the shop, but Esmé seems reluctant. After a beat, not quite able to believe what he is doing, Alfie reaches his hand down. Esmé grabs it.

Laura watches the pair exit together. Alfie is totally on edge, but holds tight to Esmé nonetheless.

ESMÉ'S MOTHER (OS)
There!

Esmé's family knock Laura over as they pelt past. Esmé's mother scoops her daughter up, furious.

ESMÉ'S MOTHER
You naughty little girl! Where have you been?

Esmé squirms but her mother keeps a firm grip.

ESMÉ'S MOTHER (CONT'D)
You think you can keep running off like this? You think it's funny?

For once, Esmé is unable to respond. Alfie draws back but Esmé's mother turns on him.

ESMÉ'S MOTHER (CONT'D)
And you, stop right there! What are you doing with my daughter? (leaning in close) You try to snatch her, hmm? That's it? Jerome, get your phone!

Alfie sweats, terrified. Esmé's lower lip wobbles.

LAURA (OS)

He was taking her to security!

Everyone turns – Laura steps forward.

ESMÉ'S MOTHER

What are you saying?

LAURA

I saw everything. He was upstairs when the announcement came on—

ALFIE

I didn't hear—

LAURA

(talking over him) He was upstairs when the announcement came on. He was taking her to security. Right?

Alfie nods.

ESMÉ'S MOTHER

And you are...?

LAURA

I work in the coffee shop. (Indicates her name badge) Laura. I saw your daughter outside. Everyone else ignored her; this boy was the only one who helped!

Esmé's mother's glare reluctantly relaxes.

LAURA (CONT'D)

I followed them the whole way. He was just trying to get her back safe. I promise.

ESMÉ'S MOTHER
(to Esmé) Is this true?

Esmé wriggles, instantly cheery again.

ESMÉ
Alfie's my best friend!

ESMÉ'S MOTHER
Hm. Very well.

She places Esmé down.

ESMÉ'S MOTHER (CONT'D)
We have to go now anyway. Do you realise how late we are, all thanks to you? Come on, move!

She gives Alfie the slightest of nods before dragging Esmé away.

ESMÉ'S MOTHER (CONT'D)
(fading) And what is this contraption in your hand?

Laura steps closer to Alfie. He glances at her, confused.

ALFIE
You followed us? All this time?

LAURA
Sorry. Couldn't help myself. I always get sentimental this time of year.

Esmé turns and gives one last wave before disappearing. Alfie waves back, sighing.

LAURA (CONT'D)
That was a good thing you did.

She rubs Alfie's shoulder. His body tenses up. He tries not to react. He can't resist a slight twitch. Laura draws her hand back.

LAURA (CONT'D)

Oops, sorry!

**Harry Mason** grew up in Leicester. After a teacher described him as 'a lovely little lad, but likely to snap one day and go on a killing spree,' he decided that a career in writing would be the safest option. If that doesn't work out, well... he's still an all right waiter.

# PHIL MONTGOMERY

## The Ferryman

*An extract from a feature-length screenplay*

FADE IN:

INT. PENTHOUSE – WEST TOWER – NIGHT

A panoramic window overlooking a twinkling Liverpool city centre. Before it, the CORPSE of a middle-aged man hangs from a noose, masked by the room's half-light.

The room is pristine, still and shadowed.

A FLASH from a camera suddenly fills it with light, and we PULL OUT to reveal that it is a hive of activity as FORENSIC INVESTIGATORS pore over every detail.

Stood still amongst the movement is TRUMAN CROSS (40s). He's lean and pale, dressed in black, with corpse-like bags under his eyes.

All of the sound is muffled, as if underwater.

NORMAN (VO)
Are you afraid of death, Truman?

INT. NORMAN'S OFFICE – NIGHT

Truman's face is garbled through a fish tank's neon-blue water. His inflated eyes watch a school of tropical fish as they dart through bubbles.

NORMAN (OS)

Truman?

Truman turns to see NORMAN TAYLOR (50s), sat in a leather armchair opposite an empty couch. The light ghosts across his face, casting harsh shadows across his cheekbones.

TRUMAN

Everyone is. Aren't they?

NORMAN

I like to think that some people don't fear dying.

TRUMAN

Well sure, some people probably don't fear anything.

Truman steps away from the fish tank and paces.

NORMAN

Let's try a different tack. What do you suppose death is like?

TRUMAN

Isn't the point of this to get me to be less morbid?

NORMAN

Indulge me.

TRUMAN

OK. I always kind of thought of it like turning out a light; first you see, then you don't. Simple.

Truman waits for a response, but Norman begins scrawling mechanically into a notebook. His eyes don't move.

TRUMAN (CONT'D)

But then I got to thinking how your eyes adjust

to the darkness. And all of a sudden, you can see again.

INT. PENTHOUSE – WEST TOWER – NIGHT

Unlike before, the room is now awash with sound. Truman's pupils constrict sharply in time with another flash.

He's holding a sealed evidence bag, inside which sits an immaculate leather-bound journal. He puts it down and crosses to the corpse. The man wears a suit and shirt with no tie, and is barefoot.

Truman stares at the gap between the corpse's feet and the wooden flooring below. It's at least a metre.

He pulls aside one of the investigators.

TRUMAN
Do we have an ID?

INVESTIGATOR
Nathan Jones, thirty-five, worked for a newspaper up in Southport.

TRUMAN
Has anything in here been moved?

INVESTIGATOR
Only what we've bagged.

Truman motions towards a chair, sat against the wall.

TRUMAN
What about the chair?

INVESTIGATOR
It was there when we got here.

TRUMAN

You know the riddle about the man who hangs himself by standing on a block of ice and waiting for it to melt?

INVESTIGATOR

Yeah?

Truman points towards the floorboards.

TRUMAN

Where's the puddle?

INT. TRUMAN'S CAR – PHARMACY – NIGHT

Truman sits inside a black sedan, idling outside a side-street pharmacy. Its large neon sign casts Truman with a sickly green hue.

NORMAN (VO)

And when your eyes adjust to this darkness, what do you suppose you see?

INT. NORMAN'S OFFICE – NIGHT

Truman halts. Norman remains motionless in his chair.

TRUMAN

Nothing. Anything. I don't know, I don't exactly have the T-shirt.

NORMAN

If you manage to see it, be sure to send me a postcard. How's work?

TRUMAN

Fine.

NORMAN
Anything interesting?

TRUMAN
Interesting? Sure. Out of the ordinary? No.

NORMAN
One man's ordinary is another man's extraordinary.

TRUMAN
Tragic.

NORMAN
Perhaps you should write a book.

TRUMAN
Perhaps you should write a prescription.

Norman closes his notebook.

NORMAN
That time again, is it? How's the Paroxetine treating you?

TRUMAN
Getting by.

NORMAN
Headaches? Night terrors? Uncontrollable urge to take over the world?

TRUMAN
All of the above.

INT. TRUMAN'S CAR – PHARMACY – NIGHT

Truman rolls a bottle of pills between his fingers.

NORMAN (VO)
Let's stick with that, then. But do let me know if you actually get the urge to take over the world; I've got something else that might help with that.

Truman checks his watch.

TRUMAN
Shit.

He stows the bottle in the glovebox and shifts into gear.

INT. CLASSROOM – NIGHT

In complete silence, a TUTOR stands before a class of around a dozen attentive adult PUPILS. She's speaking in SIGN LANGUAGE. A whiteboard behind her features beginner-level translations.

Footsteps echo down the adjacent corridor until the door RATTLES open and Truman steps into the room.

TRUMAN
Sorry I'm late, I couldn't—

The tutor glares at him.

TUTOR
(signing)
No speaking, Truman! Now what do you say?

Truman freezes, staring at his impotent hands. She smiles and shakes her head, then sketches brief notations onto the whiteboard, followed by the word 'SORRY'.

Truman shuffles to the back of the class and sits.

INT. TRUMAN'S APARTMENT – LIVING ROOM – NIGHT

A small window offers a similar view over the city as the penthouse, but it's significantly cropped. The room is undecorated and cluttered with boxes.

Truman enters and lays car keys down on an empty table. He stares out of the window, then draws the curtains and steps down a narrow hallway.

INT. TRUMAN'S APARTMENT – BEDROOM – NIGHT

Truman lies flat on top of the covers. He gazes with wide eyes across the bed, then finally shuts them.

INT. PITCH BLACK ROOM

A beam of light streams in from above, illuminating a grey SHIPPING CONTAINER. Darkness surrounds the container, like it's on an empty soundstage.

Door hanging open, the container draws nearer, but its innards are cloaked in thick shadow.

Then something appears deep inside: red LEDs, barely visible at first, then crystal clear. They read '04:59'.

They flick to '05:00' along with an alarm's grating buzz.

INT. TRUMAN'S APARTMENT – BEDROOM – DAWN

Truman hits an alarm clock reading '05:00' and the buzzing stops. He rises, still fully dressed, and groans.

EXT. CROSBY BEACH – DAWN

A stagnant tide coats the shoreline. Bronze statues are submerged in the water, some to the head, giving the impression of a river of drowning men.

Truman jogs along the promenade, watching the sunrise.

He pauses at a rail and stares towards Seaforth Dock in the distance, where spinning wind turbines frame stacks of multicoloured shipping containers.

INT. POLICE STATION – EVIDENCE ROOM – DAY

Truman flashes his warrant card to an OFFICER at the room's entrance. It reads 'DETECTIVE INSPECTOR'.

Truman moves through a gate and down shelves filled with evidence boxes. Like picking a book from a library, he scans the shelves and locates the item he's looking for.

Except it's not there. His brow furrows, staring at an empty space on the shelf.

FEMALE VOICE (OS)
Sorry, you must be looking for this.

He turns and sees ALICE GOODING (mid-20s), sharply dressed, sat at a desk at the end of the shelves. An evidence box lies on the desk and her gloved hands are pressed against the leather journal from the crime scene.

ALICE
I don't have a desk yet, so I thought this would do for now.

Truman's eyes are drawn towards a cross pendant around Alice's neck, which catches the light. It sits atop her tightly-buttoned shirt. She suddenly rises and steps towards him, hand extended.

ALICE (CONT'D)
Sorry. DC Alice Gooding. I got here this

morning.

She notices the glove and snaps it off. Truman shakes her hand tentatively.

TRUMAN

Truman—

ALICE

Cross, I know. Emerson told me to come and get up to speed with a few cases; this one seemed pretty interesting.

TRUMAN

Mind if I take a look?

Without waiting for a response, Truman lifts the journal.

ALICE

It's not addressed to anyone, which is odd, I suppose. It's all very religious, which fits, but I'm not sure what point he's trying to make.

TRUMAN

Do you mind if I just read?

ALICE

No, of course.

TRUMAN

(reading, quickly)

'Why is light given to those in misery, and life to the bitter of soul – to those who long for death that does not come, and who rejoice when they can find the grave?'

ALICE

It's from Job.

TRUMAN

Job?

ALICE

The Bible.

TRUMAN

You just know that by heart?

ALICE

It's not like I could quote it or anything.

TRUMAN

And what does it mean?

ALICE

Well, he's questioning life: he wants to die but can't. It's a long time since I studied this.

TRUMAN

You still know your stuff.

Smiling, Alice lifts a stack of crime scene photos.

ALICE

The scene was cleaner than I expected. Very meticulous, again, like he's trying to make some sort of statement. But I'd have thought you'd just want to hide yourself away and never be seen again.

TRUMAN

Come again?

ALICE

If you're going to kill yourself, I mean. Why

would you care about what you leave behind?

TRUMAN
Kill himself? Right. Tell me... how do you suppose he got himself up there?

Brow furrowing, Alice takes another look at one of the photos, lost for words. Truman glances at his watch.

TRUMAN (CONT'D)
Come on. Time to find out.

INT. MORGUE – AUTOPSY ROOM – DAY

A CORONER peels back a sheet to reveal strangulation marks around the neck of the CORPSE from the crime scene. Truman stands over the autopsy table, Alice well behind.

CORONER
Cause of death is cerebral hypoxia from strangulation, as expected.

TRUMAN
Here's where you tell me it was done elsewhere and then he was strung up.

The coroner lifts the sheet over the corpse's feet, revealing deep purple bruising.

CORONER
Nothing says it, Truman. Lividity as we'd expect.

TRUMAN
Signs of a struggle?

CORONER

None.

ALICE

So it is a suicide, then?

CORONER

I can't definitively say. I don't know how he got up there, but he did. Now whether there's more to it or not is another matter, but that's for you to figure out, not me.

Jaw clenching, Truman begins to restore the sheet.

CORONER (CONT'D)

Before you do that, there's one last thing. Do either of you know of something called Charon's obol?

ALICE

Charon as in the ferryman?

CORONER

Precisely.

Truman's eyes narrow on Alice, bewildered.

TRUMAN

I'm sorry, how do you know this?

ALICE

I read.

TRUMAN

You're going to have to get me up to speed.

CORONER

In Greek mythology, Charon was responsible for carrying the newly-deceased across the River Acheron and into Hades. You're familiar with Hades?

TRUMAN
Yes, I'm familiar with Hades.

CORONER
It's said that in ancient times, people would place a coin in the mouth of the dead to pay for their passage across the river, lest the ferryman leave them stranded, doomed to wander the shores of the underworld for eternity.

ALICE
Like a religious rite.

CORONER
Yes. And that coin was called Charon's obol.

TRUMAN
And how exactly does that relate?

The coroner lifts up a POUND COIN.

CORONER
I found this in the mouth of the deceased.

Still holding the sheet, Truman peels it back a little and stares down at the corpse's mouth, shut tight.

CORONER (CONT'D)
Thing is, there's no way this would have stayed put during the act. His body would have instinctively fought for air, and you would've found this on the floor, not in his mouth.

ALICE
Meaning what?

Truman takes the coin from the coroner and holds it up, staring at it.

TRUMAN
Meaning somebody put it there.

FADE OUT.

**Phil Montgomery** is a film and television writer who works primarily in thriller and drama. He has boundless enthusiasm for photography and independent film-making and, despite his penchant for film noir, he promises that he doesn't see exclusively in black and white.

# OLIVIA WARING

## Bram's Emporium

*A pilot*

FADE IN:

EXT. MOORS – NEAR WHITBY – NIGHT

A bodiless force moves swiftly over the moorland. In the distance, Whitby Abbey stands out against the sea, beneath a full moon.

EXT. B-ROAD – OUTER WHITBY – NIGHT

A purple Nissan Micra snails along a narrow country road, moonlight bouncing off its bodywork. A Jean Michel Jarre record is audible from within.

The car moves past a signpost for Whitby. Moments later, the Micra pulls over and a body – adult male – is ejected from the passenger door. It convulses on the ground.

The car moves off.

CUT TO:

TITLES OVER BLACK

EXT. WHITBY – DAY

Late November. Waves lash at the beach. Blackbirds circle the Abbey.

EXT. PARADE OF SHOPS – WHITBY – DAY

A row of touristy tat shops. Only one remains open – 'BRAM'S EMPORIUM – Purveyors of Curiosities' – though you wouldn't know it. The 'OPEN' sign is minuscule and velvet drapes conceal the interior.

A yellow mobility scooter halts out front. On it sits IVAN (50), officious and bumbling, wearing a flat cap, a yellow waterproof gilet and a bumbag. He has a deformity: his arms are half the length of the male average.

Ivan climbs off, carrying a shopping bag, and secures his vehicle to a drainpipe. The door releases a hollow wail as he enters.

INT. SHOP – BRAM'S EMPORIUM – WHITBY – DAY

Dead silence.

Three red ten watt bulbs cast a gloomy glow on the shop. Ivan takes a small torch out of his gilet pocket, turns it on and begins moving through, whistling.

Curtained cabinets flank one wall, containing a variety of gothic curios. The other half of the shop proffers an array of familiar joke shop items. But the halloween masks are horribly real.

Ivan is approaching the counter when he hears a gutteral Yorkshire growl.

CRISPIN

Turn that off.

The torch light travels slowly up. It hits the sallow face of Ivan's landlord CRISPIN CROCKETT (55), a Jeremy Kyle Rasputin in inch-thick specs.

IVAN
I don't want to break my neck in here.

CRISPIN
Shall I do the honours, then?

Ivan switches the torch off, plonks the plastic bag on the counter and shuffles through a black curtain behind Crispin.

Out of the bag Crispin lifts the items: four cans of spray paint and four packs of beef mince. He examines them. Sighs.

INT. KITCHEN – BRAM'S EMPORIUM – WHITBY – DAY

A pokey, grotty kitchen. The fruit bowl is concealed by furry mould. The fridge looks to have passed its Silver Jubilee.

Crispin comes through the curtain holding the mince. Ivan is grazing in a bag of Bombay mix.

CRISPIN
I asked for lamb mince. It's more biblical.

IVAN
More expensive in't it?

Crispin sits, opens the mince, and pokes it with his finger.

IVAN (CONT'D)
Eh, I found something for the shop.

From his bumbag, Ivan lifts out a six-inch-high plastic toilet. On the lid are the words 'MYSTERY BOG' and there is a button with 'PRESS HERE' printed on it.

IVAN (CONT'D)
Cancer Research. Fifty pence. Daylight robbery!

Ivan cannot resist a demonstration, and excitedly presses the button himself. A skeletal hand reaches out from under the lid then retreats.

IVAN (CONT'D)
Gotta love that.

CRISPIN
We don't sell this kind of bollocks in the emporium. Get back in your hovel.

IVAN
Oh, that reminds me. The draught in my room is becoming bloody ridiculous. The windows rattle all night. Anyway I was gonna ask...

A long creak. What appeared to be the fridge door opens up. Out of it walks MARILYN (19), Crispin's adopted daughter.

She is a ghostly Jean Harlow, with a Kendal Mint Cake complexion and scarlet lips, wearing a blue dress with a white puritan-style collar.

In her hand she holds a mug with 'I ♥ DAD' on it. She pours in blackcurrant squash.

IVAN (CONT'D)
Morning, Marilyn.

Crispin begins laying the mince out on the tabletop.

IVAN (CONT'D)
As I was saying, my windows. Energy efficiency doesn't come into it. If it weren't for my hot water bottle I'd have frozen to death by now. Wouldn't be able to pay my rent then, would I? So I would appreciate it if you had a look at them.

CRISPIN
Did you finish the new batch, 23?

MARILYN
Yes, 77.

She pours boiled kettle water into her squash and starts drinking it. Crimson droplets slither down her chin.

Ivan gestures at the table.

IVAN
Is that hygienic?

CRISPIN
Is that what your poor mother said when they handed you over?

Crispin chuckles and looks to Marilyn for a laugh. She just stares blankly back at him.

CRISPIN (CONT'D)
Best get your brood priced up, 57.

Marilyn exits through the fridge door.

Ivan removes an old anti-bacterial cleaner from the cupboard, coats the meat and heads out of the room. Crispin starts massaging the mince with his fingers.

A buzzing alarm sounds. A red light flashes on the wall. Standing, Crispin wipes his hands on his trousers and heads back through the curtain.

INT. SHOP – BRAM'S EMPORIUM – WHITBY – DAY

A Whitby lad with a cap pushed low over his face stands in the middle of the shop holding his smartphone. We will come to know him as NED SPANNERTHORPE (23). Crispin waits, scratching the wood desk.

NED

Can I use your internet, mate?

Crispin indicates a painted sign reading 'THIS IS A WI-FI FREE ZONE.'

NED

Free Wi-Fi? Top banana. Need to tweet a photo of my stool for a Poundland discount.

Crispin hits a button under his desk. Two pipes on either side of Ned release jets of stinky fumes.

Ned splutters. Crispin grabs a towel to cover his face.

CRISPIN

Leave now, limaceous underkind.

INT. MARILYN'S ROOM – BRAM'S EMPORIUM – WHITBY – CONTINUOUS

A dingy box room featuring peeling wallpaper, framed horror film stills and strange little knick-knacks.

On a side table, there appears to be a line of cocaine. The box next to it reveals it is really crushed Tic Tacs.

Marilyn sits on her bed, picking her gums with a toothpick. She is surrounded by fanged golliwogs wearing custom vampire capes. She has been making their price tags.

At the foot of her bed are two television screens: one showing Carpenter's *The Thing*, the other showing a CCTV feed from the shop. She watches Ned run out of the door away from the fumes, before going back to her work.

EXT. PARADE OF SHOPS – WHITBY – DAY

Ned bursts out of the Emporium, coughing hard. He kicks Ivan's mobility scooter and heads off.

An Austin Metro drives past him and parks up a little way down from Bram's. Out of the driver's seat climbs STUART (40), smart but weary, desperate for a fag. He clearly does not belong here.

He talks into a mobile phone with a Southern accent.

STUART
Diane, I'm telling you, just give her a lorazepam and a pink wafer. I'll sort it out when I get there... Yes, April's left me. But you know, I am young, free and single, so. Swings and roundabouts... Monkey bars? It's an expression... No, I didn't stop at Trowell services. Goodbye, Diane. Yeah. Yep.

He hangs up.

Glancing up and down the deserted street, Stuart walks up to the railing overlooking the bay and hurriedly lights a Pall Mall. He puffs languidly and exhales.

LADY
D'you smoke, love?

Stuart nearly jumps. As if by magic, a small and rotund LADY (70) in a pink waterproof coat has appeared next to him.

STUART
Sorry. Do you want a cigarette?

LADY
I don't wanna trouble you, flower.

STUART

No, no it's fine. Don't mention it.

Stuart lights her a cigarette.

LADY

Ta, love.

The lady wobbles away fast. When Stuart looks back, she has gone.

Stuart continues smoking, and does not notice the purple Nissan Micra turn on to the high street.

The car zooms down the road. As it passes, its wing mirror collides with Stuart's. He turns at the bang.

STUART

Oi!

Stuart marches over to inspect the damage as the Micra disappears round the corner. He peers at the cracked glass. His splintered reflection stares back at him.

STUART (CONT'D)

Wonderful.

INT. GRAEME'S CAR – WHITBY – DAY

Rubbery-faced, wearing a shirt printed with rabbits, GRAEME (47) drives through the town. He is blasting out Teach-In's Eurovision hit *Ding-a-Dong*, singing and bopping along with worrying abandon.

EXT. PARKIN REST HOME – WHITBY – DAY

Graeme pulls up outside a nursing home. The sign reads: 'Parkin Rest Home – Caring for your loved ones'. Someone has crossed out 'for your loved ones' and added 'BECAUSE YOU DON'T' in marker pen.

He climbs out, carrying a briefcase, mic and amp. On the car's bumper are the words 'GRAEME PARSONS – LOCAL PERSONALITY and ILLUSIONIST to the GERIATRICS of NORTH YORKSHIRE.'

Graeme wiggles his way into the building.

The purple Micra is parked a few spaces down from his car.

INT. RELAXATION ROOM – PARKIN REST HOME – WHITBY – DAY

A dozen elderly inmates sit around on stained, threadbare armchairs.

A nurse, JOAN (44), skeletal with tattooed-on eyebrows, watches them from the doorway. She is Crispin's ex-wife.

Out of a tupperware box she takes a large cream cake and starts eating it. One of the old women, BETTY (86), snaps out of her stupor.

BETTY

That looks nice, Joan.

JOAN

It is.

BETTY

Do you think I could have one?

JOAN

No.

Graeme appears next to Joan.

GRAEME

I'm so sorry, I was updating the Cumberbatch blog and Pam had an attack. I got here as soon as I could. What's the situation?

JOAN
Well, Brian's still dead, Graeme.

GRAEME
How did he go?

JOAN
Suicide. By not going to the toilet. Took him months. He was a stupid sod but you've got to applaud the tenacity. Found him myself, four a.m. this morning.

GRAEME
Crikey.

JOAN
I wanted to ring the *Yorkshire Post* but Diane said they won't pay us or owt.

GRAEME
You should try *Take A Break*.

JOAN
Yeah, 'appen I will. A big fan of your tricks, though, was Brian.

GRAEME
Right. Well, I'll do my best to cheer them up.

JOAN
You're not Jesus, Graeme. Look at them. If a bomb went off in here they'd still call it euthanasia.

Joan hands Graeme an envelope.

JOAN
Here's your pony. Brian weren't a rich man.

Joan walks off. Graeme smiles round at his audience.

INT. FISH 'N' CHIPS RESTAURANT – WHITBY – DAY

A greasy joint with plastic table units. Spitting fat and torrential rain hitting the windows provide an unsettling ambience.

The only customers are Ned's sister FAY (18) and his girlfriend JOCASTA (18), sharing chips and examining the pictures in a gossip magazine.

FAY

Oh my God, look at her calves. They're like turkey drummers.

JOCASTA

I just want a Skeggy-ready bod. Ned says he won't be happy till he can eat off me like a big plate. You know, make a Ploughman's on me rib cage or sommat. Or a Rustler's.

They look up. Marilyn, in full chippy uniform complete with hat, stands by their table. She tears a page out of the magazine, stuffs it in her mouth and swallows.

Before the girls can react, the shop door bangs open. Stuart enters and shakes out his wind-warped umbrella.

He notices Marilyn gazing at him.

STUART

Wretched day. Do you do Pukka Pies?

She continues to eyeball him silently. Stuart is disturbed and entranced. Time seems to slow down as he lists pastries.

STUART

Cheese lattice? Chicken and mushroom slice? Steak bake? Lamb—

JOCASTA

There's a Greggs up t'road.

STUART

Thank you.

Flustered, Stuart exits and dashes off.

INT. MORGUE – POLICE STATION – WHITBY – DAY

A narrow basement room, washed blue by strip lighting.

The corpse previously abandoned by the Nissan Micra lies face-up on a trolley, emaciated with eyes frozen wide. The skin is pale grey.

PC GERTIE SHOE (30), plump and clammy, stands by the wall. The faint hum of a Take That track can be heard through her iPod headphones.

GERTIE'S POV:

The corpse's thick blackish veins seem to throb under the lights.

The whites of its eyes are yellow.

There are deep cuts on the hands, and there is grisly fingernail damage.

Its feet are curled right over.

BACK TO SCENE:

Crunch. Gertie has a pack of Quavers out and is munching listlessly.

**Olivia Waring** would ideally like to make more people squirm with her writing. The Hove-dwelling freelance journalist writes for radio, stage and screen. She is currently working on an animated black comedy series, *Wonk*, to tide her over until that beaded-curtain-panel-that-looks-exactly-like-a-door concept earns her billions.